Battle Hymn
of the Tiger Mother

ALSO BY AMY CHUA

Day of Empire: How Hyperpowers Rise to
Global Dominance—and Why They Fall

World on Fire: How Exporting Free Market Democracy
Breeds Ethnic Hatred and Global Instability

Battle Hymn
of the Tiger Mother

AMY CHUA

BLOOMSBURY

LONDON · BERLIN · NEW YORK · SYDNEY

First published in Great Britain, 2011

Copyright © Amy Chua, 2011

The moral right of the author has been asserted

Portions of Chapter Four first appeared as "On Becoming American" in *Defining a Nation: Our America and the Sources of Its Strength,* edited by David Halberstam (National Geographic, 2003).

All photographs are from the author's family collection, with the following exceptions:
p. 30, Bachrach Photography
p. 168, © Susan Bradley Photography
pp. 216 & 223, Peter Z. Mahakian

Bloomsbury Publishing Plc
36 Soho Square
London W1D 3QY

www.bloomsbury.com

Bloomsbury Publishing, London, Berlin, New York and Sydney
A CIP catalogue record for this book is available from the British Library

ISBN 978 1 4088 1267 9 (hardback edition)

ISBN 978 1 4088 1316 4 (trade paperback edition)

10 9 8 7 6 5 4 3 2

Designed by Nicole Laroche

Printed in Great Britain by Clays Ltd, St Ives Plc

For Sophia and Louisa

And for Katrin

Contents

Part One

Part Two

Part Three

This is a story about a mother, two daughters, and two dogs. It's also about Mozart and Mendelssohn, the piano and the violin, and how we made it to Carnegie Hall.

This was *supposed* to be a story of how Chinese parents are better at raising kids than Western ones.

But instead, it's about a bitter clash of cultures, a fleeting taste of glory, and how I was humbled by a thirteen-year-old.

Part One

The Tiger, the living symbol of strength and power, generally inspires fear and respect.

I

The Chinese Mother

A lot of people wonder how Chinese parents raise such stereo-typically successful kids. They wonder what these parents do to produce so many math whizzes and music prodigies, what it's like inside the family, and whether they could do it too. Well, I can tell them, because I've done it. Here are some things my daughters, Sophia and Louisa, were never allowed to do:

- attend a sleepover
- have a playdate
- be in a school play
- complain about not being in a school play
- watch TV or play computer games
- choose their own extracurricular activities
- get any grade less than an A

- not be the #1 student in every subject except gym and drama
- play any instrument other than the piano or violin
- not play the piano or violin.

I'm using the term "Chinese mother" loosely. I recently met a supersuccessful white guy from South Dakota (you've seen him on television), and after comparing notes we decided that his working-class father had definitely been a Chinese mother. I know some Korean, Indian, Jamaican, Irish, and Ghanaian parents who qualify too. Conversely, I know some mothers of Chinese heritage, almost always born in the West, who are *not* Chinese mothers, by choice or otherwise.

I'm also using the term "Western parents" loosely. Western parents come in all varieties. In fact, I'll go out on a limb and say that Westerners are far more diverse in their parenting styles than the Chinese. Some Western parents are strict; others are lax. There are same-sex parents, Orthodox Jewish parents, single parents, ex-hippie parents, investment banker parents, and military parents. None of these "Western" parents necessarily see eye to eye, so when I use the term "Western parents," of course I'm not referring to all Western parents—just as "Chinese mother" doesn't refer to all Chinese mothers.

All the same, even when Western parents think they're being strict, they usually don't come close to being Chinese mothers. For example, my Western friends who consider themselves strict make their children practice their instruments thirty minutes every day. An hour at most. For a Chinese mother, the first hour is the easy part. It's hours two and three that get tough.

Despite our squeamishness about cultural stereotypes, there are tons of studies out there showing marked and quantifiable differences between Chinese and Westerners when it comes to parenting. In one study of 50 Western American mothers and 48 Chinese immigrant mothers, almost 70% of the Western mothers said either that "stressing academic success is not good for children" or that "parents need to foster the idea that learning is fun." By contrast, roughly 0% of the Chinese mothers felt the same way. Instead, the vast majority of the Chinese mothers said that they believe their children can be "the best" students, that "academic achievement reflects successful parenting," and that if children did not excel at school then there was "a problem" and parents "were not doing their job." Other studies indicate that compared to Western parents, Chinese parents spend approximately ten times as long every day drilling academic activities with their children. By contrast, Western kids are more likely to participate in sports teams.

This brings me to my final point. Some might think that the American sports parent is an analog to the Chinese mother. This is so wrong. Unlike your typical Western overscheduling soccer mom, the Chinese mother believes that (1) schoolwork always comes first; (2) an A-minus is a bad grade; (3) your children must be two years ahead of their classmates in math; (4) you must never compliment your children in public; (5) if your child ever disagrees with a teacher or coach, you must always take the side of the teacher or coach; (6) the only activities your children should be permitted to do are those in which they can eventually win a medal; and (7) that medal must be gold.

2

Sophia

Sophia

Sophia is my firstborn daughter. My husband, Jed, is Jewish, and I'm Chinese, which makes our children Chinese-Jewish-American, an ethnic group that may sound exotic but actually forms a majority in certain circles, especially in university towns.

Sophia's name in English means "wisdom," as does Si Hui, the Chinese name my mother gave her. From the moment Sophia was born, she displayed a rational temperament and exceptional powers of concentration. She got those qualities from her father. As an infant Sophia quickly slept through the night, and cried only if it achieved a purpose. I was struggling to write a law article at the time—I was on leave from my Wall Street law firm and desperate to get a teaching job so I wouldn't have to go back—and at two months Sophia understood this. Calm and contemplative, she basically slept, ate, and watched me have writer's block until she was a year old.

Sophia was intellectually precocious, and at eighteen months she knew the alphabet. Our pediatrician denied that this was neurologically possible, insisting that she was only mimicking sounds. To prove his point, he pulled out a big tricky chart, with the alphabet disguised as snakes and unicorns. The doctor looked at the chart, then at Sophia, and back at the chart. Cunningly, he pointed to a toad wearing a nightgown and a beret.

"*Q*," piped Sophia.

The doctor grunted. "No coaching," he said to me.

I was relieved when we got to the last letter: a hydra with lots of red tongues flapping around, which Sophia correctly identified as "*I*."

Sophia excelled in nursery school, particularly in math. While the other kids were learning to count from 1 to 10 the creative American way—with rods, beads, and cones—I taught Sophia addition, subtraction, multiplication, division, fractions, and decimals the rote Chinese way. The hard part was displaying the right answer using the rods, beads, and cones.

The deal Jed and I struck when we got married was that our children would speak Mandarin Chinese and be raised Jewish. (I was brought up Catholic, but that was easy to give up.

Catholicism has barely any roots in my family, but more of that later.) In retrospect, this was a funny deal, because I myself don't speak Mandarin—my native dialect is Hokkien Chinese—and Jed is not religious in the least. But the arrangement somehow worked. I hired a Chinese nanny to speak Mandarin constantly to Sophia, and we celebrated our first Hanukkah when Sophia was two months old.

As Sophia got older, it seemed like she got the best of both cultures. She was probing and questioning, from the Jewish side. And from me, the Chinese side, she got skills—lots of skills. I don't mean inborn skills or anything like that, just skills learned the diligent, disciplined, confidence-expanding Chinese way. By the time Sophia was three, she was reading Sartre, doing simple set theory, and could write one hundred Chinese characters. (Jed's translation: She recognized the words "No Exit," could draw two overlapping circles, and okay maybe on the Chinese characters.) As I watched American parents slathering praise on their kids for the lowest of tasks—drawing a squiggle or waving a stick—I came to see that Chinese parents have two things over their Western counterparts: (1) higher dreams for their children, and (2) higher regard for their children in the sense of knowing how much they can take.

Of course, I also wanted Sophia to benefit from the best aspects of American society. I did not want her to end up like one of those weird Asian automatons who feel so much pressure from their parents that they kill themselves after coming in second on the national civil service exam. I wanted her to be well rounded and to have hobbies and activities. Not just any activity, like "crafts," which can lead nowhere—or even worse, playing the drums, which leads to drugs—but rather a hobby that was meaningful and highly difficult with the potential for depth and virtuosity.

And that's where the piano came in.

In 1996, when she was three, Sophia got two new things: her first piano lesson, and a little sister.

3

Louisa

Louisa

There's a country music song that goes, "She's a wild one with an angel's face." That's my younger daughter, Lulu. When I think of her, I think of trying to tame a feral horse. Even when she was in utero she kicked so hard it left visible imprints on my stomach. Lulu's real name is Louisa, which means "famous warrior." I'm not sure how we called that one so early.

Lulu's Chinese name is Si Shan, which means "coral" and connotes delicacy. This fits Lulu too. From the day she was born,

Lulu had a discriminating palate. She didn't like the infant formula I fed her, and she was so outraged by the soy milk alternative suggested by our pediatrician that she went on a hunger strike. But unlike Mahatma Gandhi, who was selfless and meditative while he starved himself, Lulu had colic and screamed and clawed violently for hours every night. Jed and I were in earplugs and tearing our hair out when fortunately our Chinese nanny Grace came to the rescue. She prepared a silken tofu braised in a light abalone and shiitake sauce with a cilantro garnish, which Lulu ended up quite liking.

It's hard to find the words to describe my relationship with Lulu. "All-out nuclear warfare" doesn't quite capture it. The irony is that Lulu and I are very much alike: She inherited my hot-tempered, viper-tongued, fast-forgiving personality.

Speaking of personalities, I don't believe in astrology—and I think people who do have serious problems—but the Chinese Zodiac describes Sophia and Lulu *perfectly*. Sophia was born in the Year of the Monkey, and Monkey people are curious, intellectual, and "generally can accomplish any given task. They appreciate difficult or challenging work as it stimulates them." By contrast, people born in the Year of the Boar are "willful" and "obstinate" and often "fly into a rage," although they "never harbor a grudge," being fundamentally honest and warmhearted. That's Lulu exactly.

I was born in the Year of the Tiger. I don't want to boast or anything, but Tiger people are noble, fearless, powerful, authoritative, and magnetic. They're also supposed to be lucky. Beethoven and Sun Yat-sen were both Tigers.

I had my first face-off with Lulu when she was about three. It was a freezing winter afternoon in New Haven, Connecticut, one of the coldest days of the year. Jed was at work—he was a professor at Yale Law School—and Sophia was at kindergarten. I decided that it would be a perfect time to introduce Lulu to the piano. Excited about working together—with her brown curls, round eyes, and china doll face, Lulu was deceptively cute—I put her on the piano bench, on top of some comfortable pillows. I then demonstrated how to play a single note with a single finger, evenly, three times, and asked her to do the same. A small request, but Lulu refused, preferring instead to smash at many notes at the same time with two open palms. When I asked her to stop, she smashed harder and faster. When I tried to pull her away from the piano, she began yelling, crying, and kicking furiously.

Fifteen minutes later, she was still yelling, crying, and kicking, and I'd had it. Dodging her blows, I dragged the screeching demon to our back porch door, and threw it open.

The wind chill was twenty degrees, and my own face hurt from just a few seconds' exposure to the icy air. But I was determined to raise an obedient Chinese child—in the West, obedience is associated with dogs and the caste system, but in Chinese culture, it is considered among the highest of virtues—if it killed me. "You can't stay in the house if you don't listen to Mommy," I said sternly. "Now, are you ready to be a good girl? Or do you want to go outside?"

Lulu stepped outside. She faced me, defiant.

A dull dread began seeping though my body. Lulu was wearing only a sweater, a ruffled skirt, and tights. She had stopped crying. Indeed, she was eerily still.

"Okay good—you've decided to behave," I said quickly. "You can come in now."

Lulu shook her head.

"Don't be silly, Lulu." I was panicking. "It's freezing. You're going to get sick. Come in *now*."

Lulu's teeth were chattering, but she shook her head again. And right then I saw it all, as clear as day. I had underestimated Lulu, not understood what she was made of. She would sooner freeze to death than give in.

I had to change tactics immediately; I couldn't win this one. Plus I might be locked up by Child Services. My mind racing, I reversed course, now begging, coddling, and bribing Lulu to come back into the house. When Jed and Sophia arrived home, they found Lulu contentedly soaking in a hot bath, dipping a brownie in a steaming cup of hot chocolate with marshmallows.

But Lulu had underestimated me too. I was just rearming. The battle lines were drawn, and she didn't even know it.

4

The Chuas

My last name is Chua—Cài in Mandarin—and I love it. My family comes from southern China's Fujian Province, which is famous for producing scholars and scientists. One of my direct ancestors on my father's side, Chua Wu Neng, was the royal astronomer to Emperor Shen Zong of the Ming Dynasty, as well as a philosopher and poet. Obviously wide-ranging in his skills, Wu Neng was appointed by the emperor to be the chief of military staff in 1644, when China faced a Manchu invasion. My family's most prized heirloom—in fact, our only heirloom—is a 2000-page treatise, handwritten by Wu Neng, interpreting the *I Ching*, or *Book of Changes*, one of the oldest of the classic Chinese texts. A leather-bound copy of Wu Neng's treatise—with the character for "Chua" on the cover—now sits prominently on my living room coffee table.

All of my grandparents were born in Fujian, but at different points in the 1920s and 1930s they boarded boats for the Philippines, where there was said to be more opportunity. My mother's father was a kind, mild-mannered schoolteacher who became a rice merchant to support his family. He was not religious and not particularly good at business. His wife, my grandmother, was a great beauty and devout Buddhist. Despite the antimaterialistic teachings of the Bodhisattva Guanyin, she always wished her husband were more successful.

My father's father, a good-natured fish-paste merchant, was also not religious and not particularly good at business. His wife, my Dragon Lady grandmother, made a fortune after World War II by going into plastics, then investing her profits in gold bars and diamonds. After she became wealthy—securing an account to produce containers for Johnson & Johnson was key—she moved into a grand hacienda in one of Manila's most prestigious neighborhoods. She and my uncles started buying up Tiffany glass, Mary Cassatts, Braques, and condos in Honolulu. They also converted to Protestantism and began using forks and spoons instead of chopsticks, to be more like Americans.

Born in China in 1936, my mother arrived in the Philippines with her family when she was two. During the Japanese occupation of the Philippines, she lost her infant brother, and I'll never forget her description of Japanese soldiers holding her uncle's jaws open, forcing water down his throat, and laughing about how he was going to burst like an overfilled balloon. When General Douglas MacArthur liberated the Philippines in 1945, my mother remembers running after American jeeps, cheering wildly, as U.S. troops tossed out free cans of Spam. After the war, my mother attended a Dominican high school, where she was converted to Catholicism. She eventually graduated from the

University of Santo Tomas first in her class, summa cum laude, with a degree in chemical engineering.

My father was the one who wanted to immigrate to America. Brilliant at math, in love with astronomy and philosophy, he hated the grubbing, backstabbing world of his family's plastics business and defied every plan they had for him. Even as a boy, he was desperate to get to America, so it was a dream come true when the Massachusetts Institute of Technology accepted his application. He proposed to my mother in 1960, and later the same year my parents arrived in Boston, knowing not a soul in the country. With only their student scholarships to live on, they couldn't afford heat their first two winters, and wore blankets around to keep warm. My father got his Ph.D. in less than two years and became an assistant professor at Purdue University in West Lafayette, Indiana.

Growing up in the Midwest, my three younger sisters and I always knew that we were different from everyone else. Mortifyingly, we brought Chinese food in thermoses to school; how I wished I could have a bologna sandwich like everyone else! We were required to speak Chinese at home—the punishment was one whack of the chopsticks for every English word accidentally uttered. We drilled math and piano every afternoon and were never allowed to sleep over at our friends' houses. Every evening when my father came home from work, I took off his shoes and socks and brought him his slippers. Our report cards had to be perfect; while our friends were rewarded for Bs, for us getting an A-minus was unthinkable. In eighth grade, I won second place in a history contest and brought my family to the awards ceremony. Somebody else had won the Kiwanis prize for best all-around student. Afterward, my father said to me: "Never, never disgrace me like that again."

When my friends hear these stories, they often imagine that I had a horrible childhood. But that's not true at all; I found strength and confidence in my peculiar family. We started off as outsiders together, and we discovered America together, becoming Americans in the process. I remember my father working until three in the morning every night, so driven he wouldn't even notice us entering the room. But I also remember how excited he was introducing us to tacos, sloppy joes, Dairy Queen, and all-you-can-eat buffets, not to mention sledding, skiing, crabbing, and camping. I remember a boy in grade school making slanty-eyed gestures at me, guffawing as he mimicked the way I pronounced *restaurant* (rest-OW-rant)—I vowed at that moment to rid myself of my Chinese accent. But I also remember Girl Scouts and hula hoops; roller skating and public libraries; winning a Daughters of the American Revolution essay contest; and the proud, momentous day my parents were naturalized.

In 1971, my father accepted an offer from the University of California at Berkeley, and we packed up and moved west. My father grew his hair and wore jackets with peace signs on them. Then he got interested in wine collecting and built himself a one-thousand-bottle cellar. As he became internationally known for his work on chaos theory, we began traveling around the world. I spent my junior year in high school studying in London, Munich, and Lausanne, and my father took us to the Arctic Circle.

But my father was also a Chinese patriarch. When it came

time to apply to colleges, he declared that I was going to live at home and attend Berkeley (where I had already been accepted), and that was that—no visiting campuses and agonizing choices for me. Disobeying him, as he had disobeyed his family, I forged his signature and secretly applied to a school on the East Coast that I'd heard people talking about. When I told him what I had done—and that Harvard had accepted me—my father's reaction surprised me. He went from anger to pride literally overnight. He was equally proud when I later graduated from Harvard Law School and when Michelle, his next daughter, graduated from Yale College and Yale Law School. He was proudest of all (but perhaps also a little heartbroken) when Katrin, his third daughter, left home for Harvard, eventually to get her M.D./Ph.D. there.

America changes people. When I was four, my father said to me, "You will marry a non-Chinese over my dead body." But I ended up marrying Jed, and today my husband and my father are the best of friends. When I was little, my parents had no sympathy for disabled people. In much of Asia, disabilities are seen as shameful, so when my youngest sister Cynthia was born with Down syndrome, my mother initially cried all the time, and some of my relatives encouraged us to send Cindy away to an institution in the Philippines. But my mother was put in touch with special education teachers and other parents of children with disabilities, and soon she was spending hours patiently doing puzzles with Cindy and teaching her to draw. When Cindy started grade school, my mother taught her to read and drilled multiplication tables with her. Today, Cindy holds two International Special Olympics gold medals in swimming.

A tiny part of me regrets that I didn't marry another Chinese person and worries that I am letting down four thousand years of civilization. But most of me feels tremendous gratitude for the freedom and creative opportunity that America has given me. My daughters don't feel like outsiders in America. I sometimes still do. But for me, that is less a burden than a privilege.

5

On Generational Decline

Newborn me and my brave parents,
two years after they arrived in America

One of my greatest fears is family decline. There's an old Chinese saying that "prosperity can never last for three generations." I'll bet that if someone with empirical skills conducted a longitudinal survey about intergenerational performance, they'd find a remarkably common pattern among Chinese immigrants fortunate enough to have come to the United States as graduate students or skilled workers over the last fifty years. The pattern would go something like this:

- The immigrant generation (like my parents) is the hardest-working. Many will have started off in the United States almost penniless, but they will work nonstop until they become successful engineers, scientists, doctors, academics, or businesspeople. As parents, they will be extremely strict and rabidly thrifty. ("Don't throw out those leftovers! Why are you using so much dishwasher liquid? You don't need a beauty salon—I can cut your hair even nicer.") They will invest in real estate. They will not drink much. Everything they do and earn will go toward their children's education and future.

- The next generation (mine), the first to be born in America, will typically be high-achieving. They will usually play the piano and/or violin. They will attend an Ivy League or Top Ten university. They will tend to be professionals—lawyers, doctors, bankers, television anchors—and surpass their parents in income, but that's partly because they started off with more money and because their parents invested so much in them. They will be less frugal than their parents. They will enjoy cocktails. If they are female, they will often marry a white person. Whether male or female, they will not be as strict with their children as their parents were with them.

- The next generation (Sophia and Lulu's) is the one I spend nights lying awake worrying about. Because of the hard work of their parents and grandparents, this generation will be born into the great comforts of the upper middle class. Even as children they will own many hardcover books (an almost criminal luxury from the point of view of immigrant parents). They will have wealthy friends who get paid for B-pluses. They may or may not attend private schools, but in either case they will expect expensive, brand-name clothes. Finally and most problematically, they will feel that they have individual rights guaranteed by the U.S. Constitution and therefore be much more likely to disobey their parents and ignore career advice. In short, all factors point to this generation being headed straight for decline.

Well, not on my watch. From the moment Sophia was born and I looked into her cute and knowing face, I was determined not to let it happen to her, not to raise a soft, entitled child—not to let my family fall.

That's one of the reasons that I insisted Sophia and Lulu do classical music. I knew that I couldn't artificially make them feel like poor immigrant kids. There was no getting around the fact that we lived in a large old house, owned two decent cars, and stayed in nice hotels when we vacationed. But I *could* make sure that Sophia and Lulu were deeper and more cultivated than my parents and I were. Classical music was the opposite of decline, the opposite of laziness, vulgarity, and spoiledness. It was a way for my children to achieve something I hadn't. But it was also a tie-in to the high cultural tradition of my ancient ancestors.

My antidecline campaign had other components too. Like my parents, I required Sophia and Lulu to be fluent in Chinese and to be straight-A students. "Always check your test answers three times," I told them. "Look up every word you don't know and memorize the exact definition." To make sure that Sophia and Lulu weren't pampered and decadent like the Romans when their empire fell, I also insisted that they do physical labor.

"When I was fourteen, I dug a swimming pool for my father by myself with a pick and shovel," I told my daughters more than once. This is actually true. The pool was only three feet deep and ten feet in diameter and came in a kit, but I really did dig it in the backyard of a cabin near Lake Tahoe that my father bought, after saving up for years. "Every Saturday morning," I also loved to harp, "I vacuumed half the house while my sister did the other half. I cleaned toilets, weeded the lawn, and chopped wood. Once I built a rock garden for my father, and I had to carry boulders that were over fifty pounds each. That's why I'm so tough."

Because I wanted them to practice as much as possible, I didn't ask my daughters to chop wood or dig a pool. But I did try to make them carry heavy objects—overflowing laundry baskets up and down stairs, garbage out on Sundays, suitcases when we traveled—as often as I could. Interestingly, Jed had the opposite instinct. It bothered him to see the girls loaded down, and he always worried about their backs.

In imparting these lessons to the girls, I'd constantly remember things my own parents had said to me. "Be modest, be humble, be simple," my mother used to chide. "The last shall come first." What she really meant of course was, "Make sure you come in first so that you have something to be humble about." One of my father's bedrock principles was, "Never complain or make excuses. If something seems unfair at school, just prove yourself by working twice as hard and being twice as good." These tenets too I tried to convey to Sophia and Lulu.

Finally, I tried to demand as much respect from the girls as my parents did of me. This is where I was least successful. Growing up, I was terrified of my parents' disapproval. Not so with Sophia and especially Lulu. America seems to convey something to kids that Chinese culture doesn't. In Chinese culture, it just wouldn't occur to children to question, disobey, or talk back to their parents. In American culture, kids in books, TV shows, and movies constantly score points with their snappy backtalk and independent streaks. Typically, it's the parents who need to be taught a life lesson—by their children.

6

The Virtuous Circle

Sophia's first three piano teachers were not good fits. The first, whom Sophia met when she was three, was a dour old Bulgarian woman named Elina, who lived in our neighborhood. She wore a shapeless skirt and knee-high stockings, and seemed to carry the sorrows of the world on her shoulders. Her idea of a piano lesson was to come to our house and play the piano herself for an hour, while Sophia and I sat on the couch and listened to her tortured anguish. When the first session ended, I felt like sticking my head in the oven; Sophia was playing with paper dolls. I was terrified to tell Elina it wouldn't work out, for fear that she might throw herself wailing over a parapet. So I told her we were incredibly excited about having another lesson, and that I'd contact her soon.

The next teacher we tried was a peculiar little person with short hair and round, wire-rimmed glasses named MJ, who had been in the military. We couldn't tell if MJ was male or female, but it always wore a suit and bow tie, and I liked its matter-of-fact style. MJ told us the first time we met that Sophia was definitely musically gifted. Unfortunately, MJ disappeared after three weeks. One day we arrived at MJ's house for a lesson as usual, and found no trace of MJ. Instead, there were strangers living in the house, with completely different furniture.

Our third teacher was a soft-spoken jazz guy named Richard, with wide hips. He said he had a two-year-old daughter. At our first meeting, he gave Sophia and me a big lecture about the importance of living in the moment and playing for oneself. Unlike traditional teachers, he said he didn't believe in using books written by others, and instead would emphasize improvisation and self-expression. Richard said there were no rules in music, only what felt right, and no one had the right to judge you, and the piano world had been destroyed by commercialism and cut-throat competition. Poor guy—I guess he just didn't have what it took.

As the eldest daughter of Chinese immigrants, I don't have time to improvise or make up my own rules. I have a family name to uphold, aging parents to make proud. I like clear goals, and clear ways of measuring success.

That's why I liked the Suzuki method of teaching piano. There are seven books, and everybody has to start with Book One. Each book includes ten to fifteen songs, and you have to go in order. Kids who practice hard get assigned new songs each week, whereas kids who don't practice get stuck on the same song for weeks, even months, and sometimes just quit because they're bored out of their minds. Anyway, the bottom line is that some kids go through the Suzuki books *much faster than others*. So a hardworking four-year-old can be ahead of a six-year-old, a six-year-old can be way ahead of a sixteen-year-old, and so on—which is why the Suzuki system is known for producing "child prodigies."

That's what happened with Sophia. By the time she was five, we had settled in with a fabulous Suzuki teacher named Michelle, who had a big piano studio in New Haven at a place called the Neighborhood Music School. Patient and perceptive, Michelle got Sophia—appreciated her aptitude but saw beyond it—and it was Michelle who instilled the love of music in her.

The Suzuki method was perfect for Sophia. She learned really quickly and could stay focused for a long time. She also had a big cultural advantage: Most of the other students at the school had liberal Western parents, who were weak-willed and indulgent when it came to practicing. I remember a girl named Aubrey, who was required to practice one minute per day for every year of her age. She was seven. Other kids got paid for practicing, with giant ice cream sundaes or big Lego kits. And many were excused from practicing altogether on lesson days.

A key feature of the Suzuki approach is that a parent is expected to attend every music lesson and then to supervise practice sessions at home. What this meant was that every moment Sophia was at the piano, I was there with her, and I was being educated too. I had taken piano lessons as a child, but my parents didn't have the money to hire anyone good, so I ended up studying with a neighbor, who sometimes hosted Tupperware parties during my lesson. With Sophia's teacher, I started learning all kinds of things about music theory and music history that I'd never known before.

With me at her side, Sophia practiced at least ninety minutes every day, including weekends. On lesson days, we practiced twice as long. I made Sophia memorize everything, even if it wasn't required, and I never paid her a penny. That's how we blasted through those Suzuki books. Other parents aimed for one book a year. We started off with the "Twinkle, Twinkle" variations (Book One); three months later Sophia was playing Schumann (Book Two); six months after that, she was playing a sonatina by Clementi (Book Three). And I still felt we were going too slow.

This seems like a good time to get something off my chest. The truth is, it wasn't always enjoyable for Sophia to have me as a mother. According to Sophia, here are three things I actually said to her at the piano as I supervised her practicing:

1. Oh my God, you're just getting worse and worse.
2. I'm going to count to three, then I want *musicality*!
3. If the next time's not PERFECT, I'm going to *TAKE ALL YOUR STUFFED ANIMALS AND BURN THEM!*

In retrospect, these coaching suggestions seem a bit extreme. On the other hand, they were highly effective. Sophia and I were a great mother-daughter fit. I had the conviction and the tunnel-vision drive. Sophia had the maturity, patience, and empathy I should have had, but didn't. She accepted my premise that I knew and wanted what was best for her—and she cut me a break when I was bad-tempered or said hurtful things.

When Sophia was nine, she won a local piano award, performing a piece called *Butterfly* by the Norwegian composer Edvard Grieg. *Butterfly* is one of Grieg's sixty-six Lyric Pieces, which are miniature compositions, each meant to evoke a particular mood or image. *Butterfly* is supposed to be light and carefree—and it takes hours and hours of grueling drudge-drilling to get it to sound that way.

What Chinese parents understand is that nothing is fun until you're good at it. To get good at anything you have to work, and children on their own never want to work, which is why it is crucial to override their preferences. This often requires forti-tude on the part of the parents because the child will resist; things are always hardest at the beginning, which is where Western par-ents tend to give up. But if done properly, the Chinese strategy produces a virtuous circle. Tenacious practice, practice, prac-tice is crucial for excellence; rote repetition is underrated in America. Once a child starts to excel at something—whether it's math, piano, pitching, or ballet—he or she gets praise, admira-tion, and satisfaction. This builds confidence and makes the once not-fun activity fun. This in turn makes it easier for the parent to get the child to work even more.

At the Winners Concert where Sophia performed, as I watched her deft fingers fluttering and tumbling up and down the piano like real butterfly wings, I was overcome with pride, exhilaration, and hope. I couldn't wait for the next day, to work more with Sophia, and to learn more music together.

7

Tiger Luck

Jed and me on our wedding day

Like every Asian American woman in her late twenties, I had
the idea of writing an epic novel about mother-daughter rela-
tionships spanning several generations, based loosely on my own
family's story. This was before Sophia was born, when I was living in New York, trying to figure out what I was doing working
at a Wall Street law firm.

Thank goodness I'm a lucky person, because all my life I've
made important decisions for the wrong reasons. I started off as
an applied mathematics major at Harvard because I thought it

would please my parents; I dropped it after my father, watching me struggling with a problem set over winter break, told me I was in over my head, saving me. But then I mechanically switched to economics because it seemed vaguely sciencelike. I wrote my senior thesis on commuting patterns of two-earner families, a subject I found so boring I could never remember what my conclusion was.

I went to law school, mainly because I didn't want to go to medical school. I did well at law school, by working psychotically hard. I even made it onto the highly competitive *Harvard Law Review,* where I met Jed and became an executive editor. But I always worried that law really wasn't my calling. I didn't care about the rights of criminals the way others did, and I froze whenever a professor called on me. I also wasn't naturally skeptical and questioning; I just wanted to write down everything the professor said and memorize it.

After graduating I went to a Wall Street law firm because it was the path of least resistance. I chose corporate practice because I didn't like litigation. I was actually decent at the job; long hours never bothered me, and I was good at understanding what the clients wanted and translating it into legal documents. But my entire three years at the firm, I always felt like I was playacting, ridiculous in my suit. At the all-night drafting sessions with investment bankers, while everyone else was popping veins over the minutiae of some multibillion-dollar deal, I'd find my mind drifting to thoughts of dinner, and I just couldn't get myself to care about whether the sentence

Any statement contained in a document incorporated or deemed to be incorporated by reference herein shall be deemed to be modified or superseded for purposes of this Offering Circular to the extent that a statement contained herein, or in any other subsequently filed document that also is incorporated by reference herein, modifies or supersedes such a statement.

should be prefaced by "To the best of the Company's knowledge."

Jed, meanwhile, loved the law, and the contrast made my misfit all the more glaring. At his law firm, which specialized in late-1980s takeovers, he loved writing briefs and litigating and had great successes. Then he went to the U.S. Attorney's Office and sued Mafia guys and loved that too. For fun, he wrote a 100-page article on the right of privacy—it just poured out of him—which was accepted by the same *Harvard Law Review* we'd worked on as students (which almost never publishes articles by nonprofessors). The next thing we knew he got a call from the dean of Yale Law School, and even though I was the one who always wanted to become an academic (I guess because my father was one), he got a job as a Yale law professor the year before Sophia was born. It was a dream job for Jed. He was the only junior person on the faculty, the golden boy, surrounded by brilliant colleagues who thought like he did.

I'd always thought of myself as someone imaginative with lots of ideas, but around Jed's colleagues, my brain turned to sludge. When we first moved to New Haven—I was on pregnancy leave with Sophia—Jed told his friends on the faculty that I was thinking about being a professor too. But when they asked about the legal issues I was interested in, I felt like a stroke victim. I was so nervous I couldn't think or speak. When I forced myself to talk, my sentences came out all garbled with weird words inserted in weird places.

That's when I decided to write an epic novel. Unfortunately, I had no talent for novel writing, as Jed's polite coughs and forced laughter while he read my manuscript should have told me. What's more, Maxine Hong Kingston, Amy Tan, and Jung Chang all beat me to it with their books *The Woman Warrior, The Joy Luck Club,* and *Wild Swans.* At first, I was bitter and resentful, but then I got over it and came up with a new idea. Combining my law degree with my own family's background, I would write about law and ethnicity in the developing world. Ethnicity was my favorite thing to talk about anyway. Law and development, which very few people were studying at the time, would be my specialty.

The stars were aligned. Just after Sophia was born, I wrote an article about privatization, nationalization, and ethnicity in Latin America and Southeast Asia, which the *Columbia Law Review* accepted for publication. Armed with my new article, I applied for law teaching jobs all over the country. In a mind-boggling act of temerity, I said yes when Yale's hiring committee invited me to interview with them. I met with the committee over lunch at a scary Yale institution called Mory's, and was so tongue-tied that two professors excused themselves early and the dean of the law school spent the rest of the two hours pointing out Italianate influences on New Haven architecture.

I did not get asked back to meet the full Yale Law faculty, which meant that I'd flunked the lunch. In other words, I'd been rejected by Jed's colleagues. This was not ideal—and it made socializing a little tricky.

But then I got another huge break. When Sophia was two, Duke Law School gave me a teaching offer. Ecstatic, I accepted the offer immediately, and we moved to Durham, North Carolina.

8

Lulu's Instrument

Lulu and her first violin

I loved Duke. My colleagues were generous, kind, and smart, and we made many close friends. The only hitch was that Jed still worked at Yale, which was five hundred miles away. But we made it work, alternating some years between Durham and New Haven, with Jed doing most of the commuting.

In 2000, when Sophia was seven and Lulu was four, I got a call from New York University Law School, inviting me to visit. I hated the idea of leaving Duke, but New York was a lot closer to

New Haven, so we packed up and moved to Manhattan for six months.

It was a stressful six months. To "visit" in the law teaching world is to join a faculty on a trial basis. It's basically a semester-long interview where you try to impress everyone with how smart you are while sucking up to them at the same time. ("But I have a bone to pick with you, Bertram. Doesn't your paradigm-shifting model actually have even more far-reaching implications than you thought?" Or: "I'm not sure I'm fully persuaded yet by footnote 81 of your 'Law and Lacan' article, which is downright dangerous—would you mind if I assigned it to my class?")

When it came to schools, Manhattan lived up to its hair-raising reputation. Jed and I were introduced to the world of third-graders prepping for the SAT and toddlers with trust funds and their own photography portfolios. In the end, we decided to send Sophia to a public school, P.S. 3, which was right across the street from the apartment we'd rented. For Lulu to get into preschool, though, she had to take a series of tests.

At the preschool I most wanted Lulu to get in, which was in a beautiful church with stained-glass windows, the admissions director came back out with Lulu after just five minutes, wanting to confirm that Lulu could not count—not that there was anything wrong with that, but she just wanted to confirm.

"Oh my goodness, of course she can count!" I exclaimed, horrified. "Give me just one second with her."

I pulled my daughter aside. "Lulu!" I hissed. "What are you *doing*? This is not a joke."

Lulu frowned. "I only count in my head."

"You can't just count in your head—you have to count out

loud to show the lady you can count! She is *testing* you. They won't let you into this school if you don't show them."

"I don't want to go to this school."

As already mentioned, I don't believe in bribing children. Both the United Nations and the Organisation for Economic Co-operation and Development have ratified international conventions against bribery; also, if anything, children should pay their parents. But I was desperate. "Lulu," I whispered, "if you do this, I'll give you a lollipop and take you to the bookstore."

I dragged Lulu back. "She's ready now," I said brightly.

This time, the admissions director allowed me to accompany Lulu into the testing room. She put four blocks on the table and asked Lulu to count them.

Lulu glanced at the blocks, then said, "Eleven, six, ten, *four*."

My blood ran cold. I thought about grabbing Lulu and making a run for it, but the director was calmly adding four more blocks to the pile. "How about now, Lulu—can you count those?"

Lulu stared at the blocks a little longer this time, then counted, "Six, four, one, three, zero, twelve, two, *eight*."

I couldn't stand it. "Lulu! Stop that—"

"No, no—please." The director put her hand up, an amused look on her face, and turned back to Lulu. "I can see, Louisa, that you like doing things your own way. Am I right?"

Lulu shot a furtive glance at me—she knew I was displeased—then gave a small nod.

"There *are* eight blocks," the woman went on casually. "You were correct—even if you arrived at the answer in an unusual way. It's an admirable thing to want to find your own path. That's something we try to encourage at this school."

I relaxed, finally allowing myself to breathe. The woman liked Lulu, I could tell. In fact, a lot of people liked Lulu—there was something almost magnetic about her inability to ingratiate. Thank God we live in America, I thought to myself, where no doubt because of the American Revolution rebelliousness is valued. In China, they'd have sent Lulu to a labor camp.

Ironically, Lulu ended up loving her New York school, while Sophia, who'd always been a little shy, had a harder time. At our parent conference, Sophia's teacher told us that while she'd never taught a better student, she worried about Sophia socially, because she spent every lunch and recess alone, wandering around the yard with a book. Jed and I panicked, but when we asked Sophia about school, she insisted that she was having fun.

We made it through that semester in New York City, just barely. I even managed to get an offer from NYU, which I almost took. But then a series of unexpected events unfolded. I published a law review article on democratization and ethnicity in developing countries, which got a lot of attention in policy-making circles. Because of that article, Yale unrejected me, offering to make me a tenured professor. Seven years after I couldn't make it through lunch, I accepted, even though it was a little bittersweet. Nomadic no longer, Jed could finally stop commuting, and Sophia and Lulu settled once and for all into a grade school in New Haven.

By that time, Lulu had also started taking piano lessons with Sophia's teacher Michelle at the Neighborhood Music School. I felt like I was leading a double life. I would get up at five in the morning and spend half my day writing and acting like a Yale law professor, then rush back home for my daily practice sessions with my two daughters, which in Lulu's case always involved mutual threats, blackmail, and extortion.

As it turns out, Lulu was a natural musician, with close to perfect pitch. Unfortunately, she hated drilling and wouldn't concentrate during practice, preferring instead to talk about the birds outside the window or the lines on my face. Still, she progressed quickly through the Suzuki piano books and was a great performer. At recitals, she was never flawless like her sister, but what she lacked in technical precision she more than made up for with a style and musicality every bit the equal of Sophia's.

Around that time, I decided that Lulu should start a different instrument. Friends with older children had advised me that it was better to have my two daughters pursue different interests, to minimize competition between them. This made especially good sense because Sophia had really started to take off in piano, winning lots of local prizes and often being invited by teachers, churches, and community organizations to perform. Everywhere we went, Lulu had to hear raves about her sister.

Naturally the question arose as to what new instrument Lulu should pick up. My in-laws, liberal intellectual Jews, had strong views about this. They knew of Lulu's headstrong personality and had overheard the screaming and yelling during our practice sessions. They urged me to go with something low-pressure.

"How about the recorder?" my father-in-law, Sy, suggested. A big strapping man who looks exactly like Zeus, Sy had a thriving psychotherapy practice in Washington, D.C. He's actually very musical, with a powerful, deep voice. In fact, Jed's sister also has a beautiful voice, suggesting which side of the family Sophia and Lulu got their musical genes from.

"The *recorder?*" my mother-in-law, Florence, asked, incredulous, when she heard about Sy's suggestion. "How boring." Florence was an art critic who lived in New York City. She had recently published a biography of Clement Greenberg, the controversial critic of modern art who effectively discovered Jackson Pollock and American abstract expressionism. Florence and Sy had been divorced for twenty years, and she generally didn't agree with anything he said. "How about something more exciting, like a gamelan instrument? Could she learn to play the gong?"

Florence was elegant, adventurous, and cosmopolitan. Years before, she had traveled to Indonesia, where she was captivated by the Javanese gamelan, a small orchestra of perhaps fifteen to twenty musicians who sit cross-legged on the floor and play percussive instruments like the *kempul* (a set of hanging gongs of different pitches), the *saron* (a big metal xylophone), or the *bonang* (a bunch of kettles that are played like drums but sound more like chimes).

Interestingly, the French composer Claude Debussy had the same reaction to the gamelan orchestra as my mother-in-law. For Debussy, as for Florence, the gamelan was a revelation. He wrote to a friend in 1895 that Javanese music was "able to express every shade of meaning, even unmentionable shades." He later published an article describing the Javanese as "wonderful peoples who learn music as easily as one learns to breathe. Their school consists of the eternal rhythm of the sea, the wind in the leaves, and a thousand other tiny noises, which they listen to with great care, without ever having consulted any of those dubious treatises."

Personally, I think Debussy was just going through a phase, fetishizing the exotic. The same thing happened to Debussy's fellow Frenchmen Henri Rousseau and Paul Gauguin, who started painting Polynesian natives all the time. A particularly disgusting variation of this phenomenon can be found in modern-day California: men with Yellow Fever, who date only Asian women—sometimes dozens in a row—no matter how ugly or which kind of Asian. For the record, Jed did not date any Asian women before me.

Maybe the reason I can't appreciate gamelan music, which I heard when we visited Indonesia in 1992, is that I fetishize difficulty and accomplishment. I don't know how many hundreds of times I've yelled at Lulu, "Everything valuable and worthwhile is difficult! Do you know what I went through to get this job at Yale?" Gamelan music is mesmerizing because it is so simple, unstructured, and repetitious. By contrast, Debussy's brilliant compositions reflect complexity, ambition, ingenuity, design, conscious harmonic exploration—and yes, gamelan influences, at least in some of his works. It's like the difference between a bamboo hut, which has its charm, and the Palace of Versailles.

In any case, I rejected the gong for Lulu, as I did the recorder. My instinct was just the opposite of my in-laws'. I believed that the only way for Lulu to get out from under the shadow of her high-performing sister was to play an even more difficult, more virtuosic instrument. That's why I chose the violin. The day I made that decision—without consulting Lulu, ignoring the advice of everyone around me—was the day I sealed my fate.

9

The Violin

One jarring thing that many Chinese people do is openly compare their children. I never thought this was so bad when I was growing up, because I always came off well in the comparison. My Dragon Lady grandmother—the rich one, on my father's side—egregiously favored me over all my sisters. "Look how flat that one's nose is," she would cackle at family gatherings, pointing at one of my siblings. "Not like Amy, who has a fine, high-bridged nose. Amy looks like a Chua. That one takes after her mother's side of the family and looks like a monkey."

Admittedly, my grandmother was an extreme case. But Chinese people do similar things all the time. I was recently at a Chinese medicine store, and the owner told me that he had a six-year-old daughter and a five-year-old son. "My daughter," he said, "she smart. Only one problem: not *focused*. My son—he not smart. My daughter smart." Another time, my friend Kathleen was at a tennis tournament and fell into conversation with a Chinese mother who was watching her daughter play a match. The mother told Kathleen that her daughter, who was a student at Brown, was probably going to lose. "This daughter so *weak,*" she said, shaking her head. "Her older sister—much better. She go to Harvard."

I know now that parental favoritism is bad and poisonous. But in defense of the Chinese, I have two points. First, parental favoritism can be found in all cultures. In Genesis, Isaac favors Esau, whereas Rebekah loves Jacob better. In the Grimm Brothers' fairy tales, there are always three siblings—and they are never treated equally. Conversely, not all Chinese practice favoritism. In *The Five Chinese Brothers,* there is no indication that the mother loves the son who swallows the sea any more than the son with the iron neck.

Second, I don't believe that all parental comparisons are invidious. Jed is constantly criticizing me for comparing Sophia and Lulu. And it's true that I've said things to Lulu like, "When I tell Sophia to do something, she responds instantly. That's why she improves so fast." But Westerners misunderstand. When I say such things I'm not favoring Sophia; just the opposite, I'm expressing confidence in Lulu. I believe that she can do anything Sophia can do and that she's strong enough to handle the truth. I also know that Lulu compares herself to Sophia anyway. That's why I'm sometimes so harsh with her. I won't let her indulge her own inner doubts.

That's also why, on the morning of Lulu's first violin lesson, before she'd even met her new teacher, I said, "Remember, Lulu, you're only six. Sophia won her first Performance Prize when she was nine. I think you can win it earlier."

Lulu responded badly to this, saying that she hated competitions and that she didn't even want to play the violin. She refused to go to the lesson. I threatened her with a spanking and no dinner—which, back then, still worked—and finally got her to the Neighborhood Music School, where we were saved by Mr. Carl Shugart, the Suzuki violin teacher to whom Lulu had been assigned.

Mr. Shugart, about fifty with preppy good looks and thinning blond hair, was one of those people who relate better to children than to adults. With parents, he was aloof and awkward; he could barely look us in the eye. But he was a genius with children: relaxed, witty, inspirational, and fun. He was like the Pied Piper of the Neighborhood Music School, and the thirty or so kids who studied with him—Lulu among them—would have followed him anywhere.

Mr. Shugart's secret was that he translated everything technical about the violin into stories or images children could understand. Instead of *legato, staccato,* or *accelerando,* he spoke of caressing the fur of a purring cat, armies of marching ants, and mice on unicycles rolling down a hill. I remember marveling at the way he taught Lulu Dvořák's famous Humoresque no. 7. After the catchy opening theme, which people all over the world hum without even knowing it, there's an almost overly sentimental second theme that's supposed to be played with tragicomic exaggerated pathos—now how do you explain *that* to a six-year-old?

Mr. Shugart told Lulu that the second theme was sad, but not sad as in someone dying. Instead he asked her to imagine that her mother promised her a big ice cream cone with two toppings if she made her bed every day for a week—and that Lulu trustingly did so. But when the week was over, her mother refused to give her the ice cream cone. Not only that, she bought a cone for Lulu's sister, who had done absolutely nothing. This clearly struck a chord with Lulu, because after that she played Humoresque so poignantly it was as if the piece had been written for her. To this day, when I hear Humoresque—you can watch Itzhak Perlman and Yo-Yo Ma playing it on YouTube—I hear the lyrics that Mr. Shugart added: "I wa-a-nt my ice cream, oh give me my ice cream; where is the ice cream you promised m-e-e?"

Amazingly, even though I had chosen the violin for Lulu, it was immediately apparent that she had a natural affinity for it. Even early on, people were constantly struck by how naturally she moved when she played and how much she really seemed to feel the music. At Mr. Shugart's recitals she always shone, and other parents would ask if music ran in our family and whether Lulu was hoping to be a professional violinist. They had no idea about the bloodbath practice sessions back home, where Lulu and I fought like jungle beasts—Tiger versus Boar—and the more she resisted, the more I went on the offensive.

Saturdays were the highlight of my week. We spent the whole morning at the Neighborhood Music School, which was always bursting with energy and the sounds of twenty different instruments. Not only did Lulu have her lesson with Mr. Shugart; she went straight from there to a group Suzuki class with him, followed by a violin-piano duo session with Sophia. (Lulu's piano lessons, which we had not abandoned, were on Fridays.) Back at home, despite the three-hour lesson block we'd just had, I would often try to sneak in an extra postlesson practice session—nothing like getting a good jump on the next week! At night, after Lulu was asleep, I read treatises about violin technique and listened to CDs of Isaac Stern, Itzhak Perlman, or Midori, trying to figure out what they were doing to sound so good.

I admit that this schedule might sound a little intense. But I felt that I was in a race against time. Children in China practice ten hours a day. Sarah Chang auditioned for Zubin Mehta of the New York Philharmonic at the age of eight. Every year some new seven-year-old from Latvia or Croatia wins an international competition playing the monstrously difficult Tchaikovsky Violin Concerto, which I couldn't wait for Lulu to get to. Besides, I was already at a disadvantage because I had an American husband who believed that childhood should be fun. Jed always wanted to play board games with the girls, or go mini-golfing with them, or worst of all, drive them to faraway water parks with danger- ous slides. What I liked best to do with the girls was to read to them; Jed and I did that every night, and it was always everyone's favorite hour of the day.

The violin is really hard—in my view, much harder to learn than the piano. First, there is the matter of holding the thing, which isn't an issue with the piano. Contrary to what a normal person might think, the violin isn't held up by the left arm; it only looks that way. According to the famous violin teacher Carl Flesch in *The Art of Violin Playing,* the violin is to be "placed on the collarbone" and "kept in place by the left lower jaw," leaving the left hand free to move around.

If you think holding something in place with your collarbone and lower left jaw is uncomfortable, you are correct. Add to this a wooden chin rest and metal clamps jutting into your neck, and the result is the "violin hickey": a rough, often irritated red blotch just under the chin, which most violinists and violists have, and even consider a badge of honor.

Then there's "intonation"—meaning how in tune you are—another reason I think the violin is harder than the piano, at least for beginners. With piano you just push a key and you know what note you're getting. With violin, you have to place your finger exactly on the right spot on the fingerboard—if you're even just 1/10 of a centimeter off, you're not perfectly in tune. Even though the violin has only four strings, it can produce 53 different notes measured by half-step increments—and infinitely more tone colors by using different strings and bowing techniques. It's often said that the violin can capture every emotion and that it's the instrument closest to the human voice.

One thing that the piano and violin have in common—with each other but also with many sports—is that you can't play extraordinarily well unless you're relaxed. Just as you can't have a killer tennis serve or throw a baseball really far unless you keep your arm loose, you can't produce a mellifluous tone on the violin if you squeeze the bow too tightly or mash down on the strings—mashing is what makes the horrible scratchy sound. "Imagine that you're a rag doll," Mr. Shugart would tell Lulu. "Floppy and relaxed, and not a care in the world. You're so relaxed your arm feels heavy from its own weight. . . . Let gravity do all the work. . . . Good, Lulu, good."

"RELAX!" I screamed at home. "Mr. Shugart said RAG DOLL!" I always tried my best to reinforce Mr. Shugart's points, but things were tough with Lulu, because my very presence made her edgy and irritable.

Once, in the middle of a practice session she burst out, "*Stop it,* Mommy. Just *stop it.*"

"Lulu, I didn't say anything," I replied. "I didn't say one word."

"Your brain is annoying me," Lulu said. "I know what you're thinking."

"I'm not thinking anything," I said indignantly. Actually, I'd been thinking that Lulu's right elbow was too high, that her dynamics were all wrong, and that she needed to shape her phrases better.

"Just turn off your brain!" Lulu ordered. "I'm not going to play anymore unless you turn off your brain."

Lulu was always trying to provoke me. Getting into an argument was a way of not practicing. That time I didn't bite. "Okay," I said calmly. "How do you want me to do that?" Giving Lulu control over the situation sometimes defused her temper.

Lulu thought about it. "Hold your nose for five seconds."

A lucky break. I complied, and the practicing resumed. That was one of our good days.

Lulu and I were simultaneously incompatible and inextricably bound. When the girls were little, I kept a computer file in which I recorded notable exchanges word-for-word. Here's a conversation I had with Lulu when she was about seven:

> A: Lulu, we're good buddies in a weird way.
> L: Yeah—a weird, terrible way.
> A: !!
> L: Just kidding (giving Mommy a hug).
> A: I'm going to write down what you said.
> L: No, don't! It will sound so mean!
> A: I'll put the hug part down.

One nice by-product of my extreme parenting was that Sophia and Lulu were very close: comrades-in-arms against their overbearing, fanatic mother. "She's insane," I'd hear them whispering to each other, giggling. But I didn't care. I wasn't fragile, like some Western parents. As I often said to the girls, "My goal as a parent is to prepare you for the future—not to make you like me."

One spring, the director of the Neighborhood Music School asked Sophia and Lulu to perform as a sister duo at a special gala event honoring the soprano opera singer Jessye Norman, who played Aida in Verdi's spectacular opera. As it happens, my father's favorite opera is *Aida*—Jed and I were actually married to the music of *Aida*'s Triumphal March—and I arranged for my parents to come from California. Wearing matching dresses, the girls performed Mozart's Sonata for Violin and Piano in E Minor. I personally think the piece was too mature for them—the exchanges back and forth between the violin and the piano didn't quite work, didn't sound like conversations—but no one else seemed to notice, and the girls were big hits. Afterward, Jessye Norman said to me, "Your daughters are so talented—you're very lucky." Fights and all, those were some of the best days of my life.

10

Teeth Marks and Bubbles

Chinese parents can get away with things that Western parents can't. Once when I was young—maybe more than once—when I was extremely disrespectful to my mother, my father angrily called me "garbage" in our native Hokkien dialect. It worked really well. I felt terrible and deeply ashamed of what I had done. But it didn't damage my self-esteem or anything like that. I knew exactly how highly he thought of me. I didn't actually think I was worthless or feel like a piece of garbage.

As an adult, I once did the same thing to Sophia, calling her garbage in English when she acted extremely disrespectfully toward me. When I mentioned that I had done this at a dinner party, I was immediately ostracized. One guest named Marcy got so upset she broke down in tears and had to leave early. My friend Susan, the host, tried to rehabilitate me with the remaining guests.

"Oh dear, it's just a misunderstanding. Amy was speaking metaphorically—right, Amy? You didn't actually call Sophia 'garbage.'"

"Um, yes, I did. But it's all in the context," I tried to explain. "It's a Chinese immigrant thing."

"But you're not a Chinese immigrant," somebody pointed out.

"Good point," I conceded. "No wonder it didn't work."

I was just trying to be conciliatory. In fact, it had worked great with Sophia.

The fact is that Chinese parents can do things that would seem unimaginable—even legally actionable—to Westerners. Chinese mothers can say to their daughters, "Hey fatty—lose some weight." By contrast, Western parents have to tiptoe around the issue, talking in terms of "health" and never ever mentioning the f-word, and their kids still end up in therapy for eating disorders and negative self-image. (I also once heard a Western father toast his adult daughter by calling her "beautiful and incredibly competent." She later told me that made her feel like garbage.) Chinese parents can order their kids to get straight As. Western parents can only ask their kids to try their best. Chinese parents can say, "You're lazy. All your classmates are getting ahead of you." By contrast, Western parents have to struggle with their own conflicted feelings about achievement, and try to persuade themselves that they're not disappointed about how their kids turned out.

I've thought long and hard about how Chinese parents can get away with what they do. I think there are three big differences between the Chinese and Western parental mind-sets.

First, I've noticed that Western parents are extremely anxious about their children's self-esteem. They worry about how their children will feel if they fail at something, and they constantly try to reassure their children about how good they are notwithstanding a mediocre performance on a test or at a recital. In other words, Western parents are concerned about their children's psyches. Chinese parents aren't. They assume strength, not fragility, and as a result they behave very differently.

For example, if a child comes home with an A-minus on a test, a Western parent will most likely praise the child. The Chinese mother will gasp in horror and ask what went wrong. If the child comes home with a B on the test, some Western parents will still praise the child. Other Western parents will sit their child down and express disapproval, but they will be careful not to make their child feel inadequate or insecure, and they will not call their child "stupid," "worthless," or "a disgrace." Privately, the Western parents may worry that their child does not test well or have aptitude in the subject or that there is something wrong with the curriculum and possibly the whole school. If the child's grades do not improve, they may eventually schedule a meeting with the school principal to challenge the way the subject is being taught or to call into question the teacher's credentials.

If a Chinese child gets a B—which would never happen— there would first be a screaming, hair-tearing explosion. The devastated Chinese mother would then get dozens, maybe hundreds of practice tests and work through them with her child for as long as it takes to get the grade up to an A. Chinese parents demand perfect grades because they believe that their child can get them. If their child doesn't get them, the Chinese parent assumes it's because the child didn't work hard enough. That's why the solution to substandard performance is always to excoriate, punish, and shame the child. The Chinese parent believes that their child will be strong enough to take the shaming and to improve from it. (And when Chinese kids do excel, there is plenty of ego-inflating parental praise lavished in the privacy of the home.)

Second, Chinese parents believe that their kids owe them everything. The reason for this is a little unclear, but it's probably a combination of Confucian filial piety and the fact that the parents have sacrificed and done so much for their children. (And it's true that Chinese mothers get in the trenches, putting in long grueling hours personally tutoring, training, interrogating, and spying on their kids.) Anyway, the understanding is that Chinese children must spend their lives repaying their parents by obeying them and making them proud. By contrast, I don't think most Westerners have the same view of children being permanently indebted to their parents. Jed actually has the opposite view. "Children don't choose their parents," he once said to me. "They don't even choose to be born. It's parents who foist life on their kids, so it's the parents' responsibility to provide for them. Kids don't owe their parents anything. Their duty will be to their own kids." This strikes me as a terrible deal for the Western parent.

Third, Chinese parents believe that they know what is best for their children and therefore override all of their children's own desires and preferences. That's why Chinese daughters can't have boyfriends in high school and why Chinese kids can't go to sleep-away camp. It's also why no Chinese kid would ever dare say to their mother, "I got a part in the school play! I'm Villager Number Six. I'll have to stay after school for rehearsal every day from 3:00 to 7:00, and I'll also need a ride on weekends." God help any Chinese kid who tried that one.

Don't get me wrong: It's not that Chinese parents don't care about their children. Just the opposite. They would give up any-thing for their children. It's just an entirely different parenting model. I think of it as Chinese, but I know a lot of non-Chinese parents—usually from Korea, India, or Pakistan—who have a very similar mind-set, so it may be an immigrant thing. Or maybe it's the combination of being an immigrant and being from cer-tain cultures.

Jed was raised on a very different model. Neither of his par-ents were immigrants. Both Sy and Florence were born and raised near Scranton, Pennsylvania, in strict Orthodox Jewish households. Both lost their mothers at a young age, and both had oppressive, unhappy childhoods. After they were married, they got out of Pennsylvania as fast as they could, eventually settling in Washington, D.C., where Jed and his older brother and sister grew up. As parents, Sy and Florence were determined to give their children the space and freedom they had been deprived of as children. They believed in individual choice and valued inde-pendence, creativity, and questioning authority.

There was a world of difference between my parents and Jed's. Jed's parents gave him a choice about whether he wanted to take violin lessons (which he declined and now regrets) and thought of him as a human being with views. My parents didn't give me any choices, and never asked for my opinion on anything. Every year, Jed's parents let him spend the entire summer having fun with his brother and sister at an idyllic place called Crystal Lake; Jed says those were some of the best times of his life, and we try to bring Sophia and Lulu to Crystal Lake when we can. By contrast, I had to take computer programming—I hated sum-mers. (So did Katrin, my seven-years-younger sister and soul mate, who on top of computer programming read grammar books and taught herself sentence diagramming to pass the time.) Jed's parents had good taste and collected art. My parents didn't. Jed's parents paid for some but not all of his education. My parents always paid for everything, but fully expect to be cared for and treated with respect and devotion when they get old. Jed's parents never had such expectations.

Jed's parents often vacationed without their kids. They traveled with friends to dangerous places like Guatemala (where they were almost kidnapped), Zimbabwe (where they went on safari), and Borobudur, Indonesia (where they heard the gamelan). My parents never went on vacation without their four kids, which meant we had to stay in some really cheap motels. Also, having grown up in the developing world, my parents wouldn't have gone to Guatemala, Zimbabwe, or Borobudur if someone paid them; they took us to Europe instead, which has governments.

Although Jed and I didn't explicitly negotiate the issue, we basically ended up adopting the Chinese parenting model in our household. There were several reasons for this. First, like many mothers, I did most of the parenting, so it made sense that my parenting style prevailed. Even though Jed and I had the same job and I was just as busy as he was at Yale, I was the one who oversaw the girls' homework, Mandarin lessons, and all their piano and violin practicing. Second, totally apart from my views, Jed favored strict parenting. He used to complain about households where the parents never said no to their children— or, worse, said no but then didn't enforce it. But while Jed was good at saying no to the girls, he didn't have an affirmative plan for them. He would never have forced things like piano or violin on them if they refused. He wasn't absolutely confident that he could make the right choices for them. That's where I came in.

But probably most important, we stuck with the Chinese model because the early results were hard to quarrel with. Other parents were constantly asking us what our secret was. Sophia and Lulu were model children. In public, they were polite, interesting, helpful, and well spoken. They were A students, and Sophia was two years ahead of her classmates in math. They were fluent in Mandarin. And everyone marveled at their classical music playing. In short, they were just like Chinese kids.

Except not quite. We took our first trip to China with the girls in 1999. Sophia and Lulu both have brown hair, brown eyes, and Asianesque features; they both speak Chinese. Sophia eats all kinds of organs and organisms—duck webs, pig ears, sea slugs—another critical aspect of Chinese identity. Yet everywhere we went in China, including cosmopolitan Shanghai, my daughters drew curious local crowds, who stared, giggled, and pointed at the "two little foreigners who speak Chinese." At the Chengdu Panda Breeding Center in Sichuan, while we were taking pictures of newborn giant pandas—pink, squirming, larvalike creatures that rarely survive—the Chinese tourists were taking pictures of Sophia and Lulu.

Back in New Haven a few months later, when I referred in passing to Sophia as being Chinese, she interrupted me: "Mommy—I'm not Chinese."

"Yes, you are."

"No, Mommy—you're the only one who thinks so. No one in China thinks I'm Chinese. No one in America thinks I'm Chinese."

This bothered me intensely, but all I said was, "Well, they're all wrong. You *are* Chinese."

Sophia had her first big music moment in 2003 when she won the Greater New Haven Concerto Competition at the age of ten, earning the right to perform as a piano soloist with a New Haven youth orchestra at Yale University's Battell Chapel. I went wild. I blew up the article about Sophia in the local newspaper and framed it. I invited more than a hundred people to the concert and planned a huge after-party. I bought Sophia her first full-length gown and new shoes. All four grandparents came; the day before the performance, my mother was in our kitchen making hundreds of Chinese pearl balls (pork meatballs covered with sticky white rice), while Florence made ten pounds of gravlax (salmon cured with sea salt under a brick).

Meanwhile, on the practice front, we kicked into overdrive. Sophia was going to perform Mozart's Rondo for Piano and Orchestra in D Major, one of the composer's most uplifting pieces. Mozart is notoriously difficult. His music is famously sparkling, brilliant, effervescent, and effortless—adjectives that strike terror in the hearts of most musicians. There's a saying that only the young and old can play Mozart well: the young because they are oblivious and the old because they are no longer trying to impress anyone. Sophia's Rondo was classic Mozart. Her teacher Michelle told her, "When you're playing your runs and trills, think of champagne or an Italian soda, and all those bubbles rising to the top."

Sophia was up to any challenge. She was an unbelievably quick study, with lightning-quick fingers. Best of all, she listened to everything I said.

By then, I had become a drill sergeant. I broke the Rondo

down, sometimes by section, sometimes by goal. We'd spend one hour focusing just on articulation (clarity of notes), then another on tempo (with the metronome), followed by another on dynamics (loud, soft, *crescendo, decrescendo*), then another on phrasing (shaping musical lines), and so on. We worked late into the night every day for weeks. I spared no harsh words, and got even tougher when Sophia's eyes filled with tears.

When the big day finally arrived, I was suddenly paralyzed; I could never be a performer myself. But Sophia just seemed excited. At Battell Chapel, when she walked out onto the stage to take her soloist's bow, she had a big smile on her face, and I could tell she was happy. As I watched her performing the piece—in the imposing dark-oak hall, she looked tiny and brave at the piano—my heart ached with a kind of indescribable pain.

Afterward, friends and strangers came up to congratulate Jed and me. Sophia's performance was breathtaking, they said, her playing so graceful and elegant. Sophia clearly was a Mozart person, a beaming Michelle told us, and she had never heard the Rondo sound so fresh and sparkling. "It's obvious that she's enjoying herself," Larry, the boisterous director of the Neighborhood Music School, said to me. "You can't sound that good if you're not having fun."

For some reason, Larry's comment reminded me of an incident from many years before, when Sophia was just starting the piano but I was already pushing hard. Jed discovered some funny marks on the piano, on the wood just above middle C. When he asked Sophia about them, a guilty look came over her. "What did you say?" she asked evasively.

Jed crouched down and examined them more closely. "Sophia," he said slowly, "could these possibly be teeth marks?"

It turned out they were. After more questioning, Sophia, who was perhaps six at the time, confessed that she often gnawed on the piano. When Jed explained that the piano was the most expensive piece of furniture we owned, Sophia promised not to do it again. I'm not quite sure why Larry's remark brought that episode to mind.

II

"The Little White Donkey"

Here's a story in favor of coercion, Chinese-style. Lulu was about seven, still playing two instruments, and working on a piano piece called "The Little White Donkey" by the French composer Jacques Ibert. The piece is really cute—you can just imagine a little donkey ambling along a country road with its master—but it's also incredibly difficult for young players because the two hands have to keep schizophrenically different rhythms.

Lulu couldn't do it. We worked on it nonstop for a week, drilling each of her hands separately, over and over. But whenever we tried putting the hands together, one always morphed into the other, and everything fell apart. Finally, the day before her lesson, Lulu announced in exasperation that she was giving up and stomped off.

"Get back to the piano now," I ordered.

"You can't make me."

"Oh yes, I can."

Back at the piano, Lulu made me pay. She punched, thrashed, and kicked. She grabbed the music score and tore it to shreds. I taped the score back together and encased it in a plastic shield so that it could never be destroyed again. Then I hauled Lulu's doll-house to the car and told her I'd donate it to the Salvation Army piece by piece if she didn't have "The Little White Donkey" perfect by the next day. When Lulu said, "I thought you were going to the Salvation Army, why are you still here?" I threatened her with no lunch, no dinner, no Christmas or Hanukkah presents, no birthday parties for two, three, four years. When she still kept playing it wrong, I told her she was purposely working her-self into a frenzy because she was secretly afraid she couldn't do it. I told her to stop being lazy, cowardly, self-indulgent, and pathetic.

Jed took me aside. He told me to stop insulting Lulu—which I wasn't even doing, I was just motivating her—and that he didn't think threatening Lulu was helpful. Also, he said, maybe Lulu really just couldn't do the technique—perhaps she didn't have the coordination yet—had I considered that possibility?

"You just don't believe in her," I accused.

"That's ridiculous," Jed said scornfully. "Of course I do."

"Sophia could play the piece when she was this age."

"But Lulu and Sophia are different people," Jed pointed out.

"Oh no, not this," I said, rolling my eyes. "Everyone is spe-cial in their special own way," I mimicked sarcastically. "Even losers are special in their own special way. Well don't worry, you don't have to lift a finger. I'm willing to put in as long as it takes, and I'm happy to be the one hated. And you can be the one they adore because you make them pancakes and take them to Yankees games."

I rolled up my sleeves and went back to Lulu. I used every weapon and tactic I could think of. We worked right through dinner into the night, and I wouldn't let Lulu get up, not for water, not even to go to the bathroom. The house became a war zone, and I lost my voice yelling, but still there seemed to be only negative progress, and even I began to have doubts.

Then, out of the blue, Lulu did it. Her hands suddenly came together—her right and left hands each doing their own imperturbable thing—just like that.

Lulu realized it the same time I did. I held my breath. She tried it tentatively again. Then she played it more confidently and faster, and still the rhythm held. A moment later, she was beaming. "Mommy, look—it's easy!" After that, she wanted to play the piece over and over and wouldn't leave the piano. That night, she came to sleep in my bed, and we snuggled and hugged, cracking each other up. When she performed "The Little White Donkey" at a recital a few weeks later, parents came up to me and said, "What a perfect piece for Lulu—it's so spunky and so *her*."

Even Jed gave me credit for that one. Western parents worry a lot about their children's self-esteem. But as a parent, one of the worst things you can do for your child's self-esteem is to let them give up. On the flip side, there's nothing better for building confidence than learning you can do something you thought you couldn't.

There are all these new books out there portraying Asian mothers as scheming, callous, overdriven people indifferent to their kids' true interests. For their part, many Chinese secretly believe that they care more about their children and are willing to sacrifice much more for them than Westerners, who seem perfectly content to let their children turn out badly. I think it's a misunderstanding on both sides. All decent parents want to do what's best for their children. The Chinese just have a totally different idea of how to do that.

Western parents try to respect their children's individuality, encouraging them to pursue their true passions, supporting their choices, and providing positive reinforcement and a nurturing environment. By contrast, the Chinese believe that the best way to protect their children is by preparing them for the future, letting them see what they're capable of, and arming them with skills, work habits, and inner confidence that no one can ever take away.

12

The Cadenza

Lulu and mean me in a hotel room (with score taped to TV)

Lulu sighed. I was driving the girls home from school, and I was in a bad mood. Sophia had just reminded me that her sixth-grade Medieval Festival was coming up, and there's nothing I hate more than all these festivals and projects that private schools specialize in. Instead of making kids study from books, private schools are constantly trying to make learning fun by having parents do all the work.

For Lulu's Passport-Around-the-World project, I had to prepare an Ecuadoran dish (chicken stewed for four hours in ground achiote, served with fried plantains), bring in Ecuadoran artifacts (a carved llama from Bolivia; no one knew the difference), and find a real Ecuadoran for Lulu to interview (a graduate student I recruited). Lulu's job was to make the passport—a piece of paper folded in quarters and labeled "Passport"—and show up for the international food festival, featuring dishes from a hundred countries, each prepared by a different parent.

But that was nothing compared to the Medieval Festival, the highlight of the sixth-grade year. For that, every student had to have a homemade medieval costume, which could not be secretly rented or look too expensive. Each student had to bring in a medieval dish prepared in an authentic medieval way. Finally, each student had to build a medieval dwelling.

So I was in a cranky mood that day, trying to figure out which architect to hire—and how to make sure it wasn't the parent of another student—when Lulu sighed again, more deeply.

"My friend Maya is so lucky," she said wistfully. "She has so many pets. Two parrots, a dog, and a goldfish."

I didn't reply. I'd been through this many times with Sophia.

"And two guinea pigs."

"Maybe that's why she's only in Book One of violin," I said. "Because she's too busy taking care of pets."

"I wish I had a pet."

"You already have a pet," I snapped. "Your violin is your pet."

I've never been much of an animal person and didn't have a pet as a child. I haven't done a rigorous empirical survey, but I'm guessing that most Chinese immigrant families in the United

States don't have pets. Chinese parents are too busy coming down hard on their kids to raise a pet. Also, they're usually tight on money—my father wore the same pair of shoes to work for eight years—and having a pet is a luxury. Finally, Chinese people have a different attitude toward animals, especially dogs.

Whereas in the West dogs have long been considered loyal companions, in China they're on the menu. This is so upsetting that it feels like an ethnic slur, but unfortunately it's true. Dog meat, especially young dog meat, is considered a delicacy in China, and even more so in Korea. I would never eat dog meat myself. I loved Lassie. Caddie Woodlawn's smart and faithful dog Nero, who finds his way back from Boston to Wisconsin, is one of my favorite literary characters. But there's a big difference between eating dog and owning one, and it never remotely occurred to me that we'd have a dog in our household. I just didn't see the point.

Meanwhile, my violin practice sessions with Lulu were getting more and more harrowing. "Stop hovering over me," she'd say. "You remind me of Lord Voldemort. I can't play when you're standing so close to me."

Unlike Western parents, reminding my child of Lord Voldemort didn't bother me. I just tried to stay focused. "Do one small thing for me, Lulu," I'd say reasonably. "One small thing: Play the line again, but this time keep your vibrato perfectly even. And make sure you shift smoothly from first position to third. And remember to use your whole bow, because it's fortissimo, with a little more bow speed at the end. Also, don't forget to keep your right thumb bent and your left pinkie curved. Go ahead—play."

Lulu would respond by doing none of the things I asked her to do. When I got exasperated, she'd say, "I'm sorry? What did you want me to do again?"

Other times when I was giving instructions, Lulu would pluck loudly at her strings as if she were playing a banjo. Or even worse, she'd start to swing her violin around like a lasso until I shouted in horror. When I told her to straighten her posture and raise her violin, she'd sometimes crumple to the floor and pretend she was dead with her tongue stuck out. And always the constant refrain: "Are we done yet?"

Yet other times, Lulu would seem to love the violin. After practicing with me, she'd sometimes want to play more by herself, and she'd fill the house with her beautiful tones, forgetting all about the time. She'd ask to bring her violin to school and come home flushed and pleased after playing for her class. Or she'd come running up to me when I was at my computer and say, "Mommy, guess what my favorite part in the Bach is!" I'd try to guess—I actually got it right about 70% of the time—and she'd either say "How did you *know*?" or "No, it's *this* part—isn't it pretty?"

If it weren't for those moments, I probably would have given up. Or maybe not. In any case, as with Sophia and the piano, I had the highest hopes for Lulu and the violin. I wanted her to win the Greater New Haven Concerto Competition so that she could play as a soloist at Battell Chapel too. I wanted her to become concertmaster of the best youth orchestra. I wanted her to be the best violinist in the state—and that was for starters. I knew that was the only way Lulu could be happy. So the more time Lulu wasted—quibbling with me, drilling halfheartedly, clowning around—the longer I made her play. "We're going to get this piece right," I'd say to her, "however long it takes. It's up to you. We can stay here until midnight if we need to." And sometimes we did.

"My friend Daniela was amazed at how much I practice," Lulu said one afternoon. "She couldn't believe it. I told her six hours a day, and she went—" And here Lulu imitated Daniela with her mouth open.

"You shouldn't have said six hours, Lulu—she's going to get the wrong idea. It's only six hours when you waste five of them."

Lulu ignored this. "Daniela felt so sorry for me. She asked when I had time to do anything else. I told her that I don't really have time for anything fun, because I'm Chinese."

I bit my tongue and said nothing. Lulu was always collecting allies, marshaling her troops. But I didn't care. In America, everyone was always going to take her side. I wasn't going to let peer pressure get to me. The few times I did, I regretted it.

Once, for example, I allowed Sophia to attend a sleepover party. This was an exception. When I was little, my mother used to say, "Why do you need to sleep at someone else's house? What's wrong with your own family?" As a parent, I took the same position, but on this occasion Sophia begged and begged me, and in a moment of uncharacteristic weakness, I finally gave in. The next morning, she came back not only exhausted (and unable to practice piano well) but crabby and miserable. It turns out that sleepovers aren't fun at all for many kids—they can be a kind of punishment parents unknowingly inflict on their children through permissiveness. After pumping Sophia for information, I learned that A, B, and C had excluded D; B had gossiped viciously about E when she was in the other room; and F at age twelve had talked all night about her sexual exploits. Sophia didn't need to be exposed to the worst of Western society, and I wasn't going to let platitudes like "Children need to explore" or "They need to make their own mistakes" lead me astray.

There are many things the Chinese do differently from Westerners. There's the question of extra credit, for example. One time, Lulu came home and told me about a math test she'd just taken. She said she thought it had gone extremely well, which is why she didn't feel the need to do the extra-credit problems.

I was speechless for a second, uncomprehending. "Why not?" I asked. "Why didn't you do them?"

"I didn't want to miss recess."

A fundamental tenet of being Chinese is that you always do all of the extra credit all of the time.

"Why?" asked Lulu, when I explained this to her.

For me this was like asking why I should breathe.

"None of my friends do it," Lulu added.

"That's not true," I said. "I'm 100% sure that Amy and Junno did the extra credit." Amy and Junno were the Asian kids in Lulu's class. And I was right about them; Lulu admitted it.

"But Rashad and Ian did the extra credit too, and they're not Asian," she added.

"Aha! So many of your friends *did* do the extra credit! And I didn't say only Asians do extra credit. Anyone with good parents knows you have to do the extra credit. I'm in shock, Lulu. What will the teacher think of you? You went to *recess* instead of doing *extra credit?*" I was almost in tears. "Extra credit is not *extra*. It's just *credit*. It's what separates the good students from the bad students."

"Aww—recess is so fun," Lulu offered as her final sally. But after that Lulu, like Sophia, always did the extra credit. Sometimes the girls got more points on extra credit than on the test itself—an absurdity that would never happen in China. Extra credit is one reason that Asian kids get such notoriously good grades in the United States.

Rote drilling is another. Once, Sophia came in second on a multiplication speed test, which her fifth-grade teacher administered every Friday. She lost to a Korean boy named Yoon-seok. Over the next week, I made Sophia do twenty practice tests (of 100 problems each) every night, with me clocking her with a stopwatch. After that, she came in first every time. Poor Yoon-seok. He went back to Korea with his family, but probably not because of the speed test.

Practicing more than everyone else is also why Asian kids dominate the top music conservatories. That's how Lulu kept impressing Mr. Shugart every Saturday with how fast she improved. "You catch on so quickly," he'd frequently say. "You're going to be a great violinist."

In the fall of 2005, when Lulu was nine, Mr. Shugart said, "Lulu, I think you're ready to play a concerto. What do you say we take a break from the Suzuki books?" He wanted her to learn Viotti's Concerto no. 23 in G Major. "If you work really hard, Lulu, I bet you can have the first movement ready for the winter recital. The only thing is," he added thoughtfully, "there's a tough cadenza in the piece." Mr. Shugart was wily, and he understood Lulu. A cadenza is a special section, usually near the end of a concerto movement, where the soloist plays unaccompanied. "It's kind of a chance to show off," said Mr. Shugart, "but it's really long and difficult. Most kids your age wouldn't be able to play it."

Lulu looked interested. "How long is it?"

"The cadenza?" said Mr. Shugart. "Oh, very long. About a page."

"I think I can do it," Lulu said. She had a lot of confidence, and, as long as it wasn't me forcing it on her, she loved a challenge.

We plunged into the Viotti, and the battles escalated. "Calm down, Mommy," Lulu would say maddeningly. "You're starting to get hysterical and breathe all funny again. We still have a month to practice." All I could think of was the work ahead of us. Although relatively simple, the Viotti concerto was a big step up from what Lulu was used to. The cadenza was filled with rapid string crossings as well as "double stops" and "triple stops"— notes played simultaneously on two or three different strings, the equivalent of chords on the piano—which were difficult to play in tune.

I wanted the cadenza to be good. It became a kind of obsession for me. The rest of the Viotti was okay—parts of it were a bit pedantic—but Mr. Shugart was right: The cadenza made the whole piece worthwhile. And about a week before the recital, I realized that Lulu's cadenza had the potential to be spectacular. She made its melodic parts sing out exquisitely; somehow that was intuitive for her. But not nearly so good were the sections that required technical precision—in particular, a series of double-stop-string-crossing zingers near the end. During practice, it was always hit or miss with those passages. If Lulu was in a good mood and concentrating, she could nail them. If she was in a bad or distracted mood, the cadenza fell flat. The worst thing was that I had no control over which mood it would be.

Then I had an epiphany. "Lulu," I said, "I have a deal to propose."

"Oh no, not again," Lulu groaned.

"This is a good one, Lulu. You'll like it."

"What—practice two hours, and I won't have to set the table? No thanks, Mommy."

"Lulu, just listen for a second. If you play the cadenza really well next Saturday—better than you've ever played it—I'll give you something you won't believe, something that *I know you will love*."

Lulu looked scornful. "You mean like a cookie? Or five minutes on a computer game?"

I shook my head. "Something so amazing even you won't be able to resist."

"A playdate?"

I shook my head.

"Chocolate?"

I shook my head again, and it was my turn to be scornful. "You think that I think you can't resist *chocolate*? I know you a little better than that, Lulu. I have in mind something you'll never EVER guess."

And I was right. She never guessed, perhaps because it was so wildly out of the realm of possibility given the available facts.

In the end, I told her. "It's a pet. A dog. If you give me a great cadenza next Saturday, I'll get us a dog."

For the first time in her life, Lulu was dumbstruck. "A . . . dog?" she repeated. "A live one?" she added suspiciously.

"Yes. A puppy. You and Sophia can decide what kind."

And that's how I outsmarted myself, changing our lives forever.

Part Two

Tigers are always tense and like to be in a hurry. They are very confident, perhaps too confident sometimes. They like being obeyed and not the other way around. Suitable careers for Tigers include advertising agent, office manager, travel agent, actor, writer, pilot, flight attendant, musician, comedian, and chauffeur.

13

Coco

Coco is our dog, my first pet ever. She's not Jed's first pet. He had a mutt called Frisky when he was a boy. Frisky, who barked a lot, was abducted and put to death by evil neighbors while Jed's family was on vacation. At least that's what Jed has always suspected. It's possible that Frisky just got lost, and was picked up by a loving Washington, D.C., family.

Technically, Coco was not Sophia and Lulu's first pet either. We had an earlier ordeal that was thankfully short-lived. When the girls were very young, Jed got them a pair of pet rabbits named Whiggy and Tory. I disliked them from the moment I saw them and would have nothing to do with them. They were unintelligent and not at all what they claimed to be. The pet-store person told Jed they were dwarf rabbits that would stay small and cute. That was a lie. Within weeks they had grown huge and fat. They moved with the gait of sumo wrestlers—they looked like sumo wrestlers—and could barely fit into their 2' x 3' cage. They also kept trying to mate with each other even though they were both males, making things very awkward for Jed. "What are they doing, Daddy?" the girls kept asking. Eventually, the rabbits mysteriously escaped.

Coco is a Samoyed, a white, fluffy dog about the size of a Siberian husky, with dark almond eyes. Samoyeds are famous for their smiling faces and lush tails that curl up over their backs. Coco has the Samoyed smile, and the dazzling pure-white Samoyed fur. For some reason Coco's tail is a little short and looks more like a pom-pom than a plume, but she's still stunningly beautiful. Although it hasn't been scientifically proven, Samoyeds are said to have descended from wolves, but in personality they are the opposite of wolves. They are sweet, gentle, friendly, loving animals, and for that reason very poor guard dogs. Originally from Siberia, they pulled sleds during the day and at night kept their owners warm by sleeping on top of them. During the winter, Coco keeps us warm in the same way. Another nice thing about Samoyeds is that they don't have dog odor. Coco smells like clean, fresh straw.

Coco was born on January 26, 2006. The runt of the litter, she has always been unusually timid. When we picked her up at the age of three months, she was a quivering white puffball. (Baby Samoyeds look like baby polar bears, and there's nothing cuter.) On the car ride back, she huddled in the corner of her crate, shaking. At home, she was too scared to eat anything. To this day, she is about 10% smaller than most Samoyeds. She is also terrified of thunder, angry voices, cats, and small vicious dogs. She still won't go down our narrow back stairs.

In other words, Coco is the opposite of the leader of the pack.

Nevertheless, not knowing a thing about raising dogs, my first instinct was to apply Chinese parenting to Coco. I had heard of dogs who can count and do the Heimlich maneuver, and the breeder told us that Samoyeds are very intelligent. I had also heard of many famous Samoyeds. Kaifas and Suggen were the lead dogs for the explorer Fridtjof Nansen's famous 1895 attempt to reach the North Pole. In 1911, a Samoyed named Etah was the lead dog for the first expedition to successfully reach the South Pole. Coco was incredibly fast and agile, and I could tell that she had real potential. The more Jed gently pointed out that she did not have an overachieving personality, and that the point of a pet is not necessarily to take them to the highest level, the more I was convinced that Coco had hidden talent.

I began to do extensive research. I bought many books and especially liked *The Art of Raising a Puppy* by the Monks of New Skete. I befriended other dog owners in my neighborhood and got helpful tips about dog parks and dog activities. I found a place that offered a Doggy Kindergarten class, a prerequisite for more advanced courses, and signed us up.

But first, there were the basics, like housebreaking. This proved more difficult than I expected. In fact, it took several months. But when we finally achieved success—Coco would run to the door and signal whenever she needed to go—it was like a miracle.

Around this time, unbelievably, an exhaustion factor started to set in with the other members of my family. Jed, Sophia, and Lulu seemed to feel that Coco had had enough training—

even though the only skill she'd mastered was not going to the bathroom anymore on our rugs. They just wanted to hug and pet Coco, and play around with her in our yard. When I looked flabbergasted, Jed pointed out that Coco could also sit and fetch and that she excelled at Frisbee.

Unfortunately, that was all Coco could do. She didn't respond to the command "Come." Worse, unless it came from Jed—who had early on demonstrated his dominance as the alpha male in the household—Coco didn't respond to the command "No," which meant that she ate pencils, DVDs, and all my nicest shoes. Whenever we had a dinner party, she'd pretend to be asleep in the kitchen until the appetizers were brought out. Then she'd dart to the living room, grab a whole pâté, and gallop around in circles, the pâté flapping and getting progressively smaller as she chomped away. Because she was so fast, we couldn't catch her.

Coco also wouldn't walk; she only sprinted at top speed. This was a problem for me, because I did all the dog walking, which in our case meant being dragged at fifty miles per hour, often straight into a tree trunk (when she was chasing a squirrel) or someone else's garage (when she was chasing a squirrel). I pointed all this out to my family, but none of them seemed concerned. "I don't have time. . . . I need to practice piano," Sophia mumbled. "Why does she need to walk?" Lulu asked.

Once, when I came back from a "walk" with my elbows scraped and my knees grass-stained, Jed said, "It's her Samoyed nature. She thinks you're a sled, and she wants to pull you. Let's forget about teaching her to walk. Why don't we just get a cart that you can sit in and have Coco pull you around?"

But I didn't want to be the neighborhood charioteer. And I didn't want to give up. If everyone else's dog could walk, why couldn't ours? So I alone took on the challenge. Following my books, I led Coco around in circles in my driveway, rewarding her with pieces of chopped steak if she didn't pull. I made ominous low sounds when she didn't obey, and high reaffirming sounds when she did. I took her for walks down half a block that lasted forever because I had to stop short and count to thirty every time the leash went taut. And finally, after all else failed, I took a tip from a fellow Samoyed owner and bought an elaborate harness that pressed against Coco's chest when she pulled.

Around that time, my glamorous friends Alexis and Jordan came to visit from Boston with their elegant sable-colored dogs, Millie and Bascha. Sisters and Australian shepherds, Millie and Bascha were the same age as Coco but smaller and sleek. Millie and Bascha were amazingly on the ball. Obviously herding dogs, they worked as a team and kept trying to herd Coco, who looks a bit like a sheep—and around Millie and Bascha, acted like a sheep. Millie and Bascha are always looking for an angle. They can do things like unlock doors and open spaghetti boxes— things that would never even occur to Coco.

"Wow," I said to Alexis that evening over drinks. "I can't believe Millie and Bascha got themselves water by turning on our garden hose. That's impressive."

"Australian shepherds are like Border collies," Alexis said. "Maybe because of their herding background, they're supposed to be really smart, at least according to the rankings on those Web sites, which I'm not sure I buy."

"Rankings? What rankings?" I poured myself another glass of wine. "How do Samoyeds rank?"

"Oh . . . I can't remember," Alexis said uncomfortably. "I think the whole idea of rating dogs by intelligence is silly anyway. I wouldn't worry about it."

The moment Alexis and Jordan left, I rushed to my computer and did an Internet search for "dog intelligence rankings." The most hits were for a list of the "10 Brightest Dogs," produced by Dr. Stanley Coren, a neuropsychologist at the University of British Columbia. I scrolled down the list, frantically looking for "Samoyed" to appear. It didn't. I found an expanded list. Samoyeds were ranked #33 out of 79—not the dumbest dog (that honor went to the Afghan hound) but definitely average.

I felt nauseated. I did further research, more targeted. To my enormous relief, I discovered it was all a mistake. According to every Web site about Samoyeds by Samoyed experts, they were extremely intelligent. The reason they didn't tend to do well on dog IQ tests is because those tests were all based on trainability, and Samoyeds are notoriously difficult to train. Why? Precisely because they are *exceptionally bright* and therefore can be obstinate. Here's a very clarifying explanation by Michael D. Jones:

> Their intelligence and strong independent nature make them a challenge to train; where a Golden Retriever, for instance, may work *for* his master, a Samoyed works *with* his master or not at all. Holding the dog's respect is a prerequisite to training.

They learn quickly; the trick is teaching the dog to behave reliably without hitting his boredom threshold. It is these characteristics that have earned Samoyeds . . . the appellation "nontraditional obedience dogs."

I discovered something else. Fridtjof Nansen, the famous Norwegian explorer—and Nobel Peace Prize winner—who almost made it to the North Pole, had conducted extensive comparative dog research before his 1895 expedition. His findings showed that "*the Samoyed surpassed other breeds* in determination, focus, endurance, and the instinctive drive to work in any condition."

In other words, contrary to "Dr." Stanley Coren's "study," Samoyeds were in fact unusually intelligent and hardworking, with more focus and determination than other breeds. My spirits soared. For me, this was the perfect combination of qualities. If the only issue was a stubborn, disobedient streak, that was nothing I couldn't handle.

One evening, after another shouting match with the girls over music, I had an argument with Jed. While he's always supported me in every way, he was worried that I was pushing too hard and that there was too much tension and no breathing space in the house. In return, I accused him of being selfish and thinking only of himself. "All you think about is writing your own books and your own future," I attacked. "What dreams do you have for Sophia, or for Lulu? Do you ever even think about that? What are your dreams for Coco?"

A funny look came over Jed's face, and a second later he burst into laughter. He came over and kissed the top of my head. "Dreams for Coco—that's really funny, Amy," he said affectionately. "Don't worry. We'll work things out."

I didn't understand what was so funny, but I was glad our fight was over.

14

London, Athens, Barcelona, Bombay

I guess I have a tendency to be a little preachy. And like many preachers, I have a few favorite themes I return to over and over. For example, there's my Anti-Provincialism Lecture Series. Just thinking about this subject makes me mad.

Whenever I hear Sophia or Lulu giggle at a foreign name—whether it's Freek de Groot or Kwok Gum—I go wild. "Do you know how ignorant and close-minded you sound?" I'll blow up at them. "Jasminder and Parminder are popular names in India. And coming from this family! What a disgrace. My mother's father's name was Go Ga Yong—do you think that's funny? I should have named one of you that. Never judge people by their names."

I don't believe my girls would ever make fun of someone's foreign accent, but maybe they would have if I hadn't preempted it. Children can be terribly cruel. "Never ever make fun of foreign accents," I've exhorted them on many occasions. "Do you know what a foreign accent is? It's a sign of bravery. Those are people who crossed an ocean to come to this country. My parents had accents—I had an accent. I was thrown into nursery school not speaking a word of English. Even in third grade, classmates made fun of me. Do you know where those people are now? They're janitors, that's where."

"How do you know?" Sophia asked.

"I think it's more important, Sophia, for you to ask yourself what it would be like if you moved to China. How perfect do you think your accent would be? I don't want you to be a provincial American. Do you know how fat Americans are? And now after 3000 years of being skinny, the Chinese in China are suddenly getting fat too, and it's because they're eating Kentucky Fried Chicken."

"But wait," said Sophia. "Didn't you say you were so fat when you were little you couldn't fit into anything in stores and your mom had to sew you clothes?"

"That's right."

"And you were so fat because you stuffed yourself with your mom's noodles and dumplings," Sophia continued. "Didn't you once eat forty-five *sio mai*?"

"I sure did," I replied. "My dad was so proud of me. That was ten more than he could eat. And three times as many as my sister Michelle could eat. She was skinny."

"So Chinese food can make you fat too," pressed Sophia.

Maybe my logic wasn't airtight. But I was trying to make a point. I value cosmopolitanism, and to make sure the girls are exposed to different cultures, Jed and I have always taken them with us everywhere we traveled—even though, when the girls were little, we sometimes had to sleep in one bed to make it affordable. As a result, by the time they were twelve and nine, the girls had been to London, Paris, Nice, Rome, Venice, Milan, Amsterdam, the Hague, Barcelona, Madrid, Málaga, Lichtenstein, Monaco, Munich, Dublin, Brussels, Bruges, Strasbourg, Beijing, Shanghai, Tokyo, Hong Kong, Manila, Istanbul, Mexico City, Cancún, Buenos Aires, Santiago, Rio de Janeiro, São Paolo, La Paz, Sucre, Cochabamba, Jamaica, Tangier, Fez, Johannesburg, Cape Town, and the Rock of Gibraltar.

The four of us looked forward to our vacations all year. Often, we'd time our trips to coincide with my parents and Cindy's trips abroad, and the seven of us would travel around together in a giant rental van driven by Jed. We'd giggle as passersby stared at us, trying to figure out our weird racial combination. (Was Jed the adopted white son of an Asian family? Or a human trafficker selling the rest of us into slavery?) Sophia and Lulu adored their grandparents, who doted on them and acted ridiculously unstrict in a way completely inconsistent with the way they'd raised me.

The girls were especially fascinated by my father, who was unlike anyone they'd ever met. He was constantly disappearing into alleys, returning with his arms full of local specialties like soup dumplings in Shanghai or *socca* in Nice. (My dad likes to try everything; at Western restaurants he often orders two main meals.) We'd always find ourselves in nutty situations: out of gas at the top of a mountain pass or sharing a train car with Moroccan smugglers. We had great adventures, and those are memories we all cherish.

There was just one problem: practicing.

At home, the girls never missed a single day at the piano and violin, not even on their birthdays or on days when they were sick (Advil) or had just had dental surgery (Tylenol-3, with codeine). I didn't see why we should miss a day when we were traveling. Even my parents were disapproving. "That's crazy," they'd say, shaking their heads. "Let the girls enjoy their vacation. A few days of not practicing won't make a difference." But serious musicians don't see it that way. In the words of Lulu's violin teacher Mr. Shugart, "Every day that you don't practice is a day that you're getting worse." Also, as I pointed out to my girls, "Do you know what the Kims will be doing while we're on vacation? Practicing. The Kims don't take vacation. Do we want them to get ahead of us?"

In Lulu's case, the logistics were easy. The violin was Lulu's airplane carry-on and fit nicely into the overhead compartment. Things were more complicated with Sophia. If we were going somewhere in the United States, a couple of long-distance phone calls usually did the trick. It turns out that American hotels are overflowing with pianos. There's typically one in the lobby bar and at least two in the various conference reception rooms. I'd just call the concierge in advance and book the Grand Ballroom at the Chicago Marriott from 6:00 A.M. to 8:00 A.M. or The Wentworth Room at the Pasadena Langham Hotel from 10:00 P.M. to midnight. Occasionally, there were glitches. In Maui, the concierge at the Grand Wailea hotel set Sophia up at an electric keyboard in the Volcano Bar. But the keyboard was two octaves too short for Chopin's Polonaise in C-sharp Minor, and there was a distracting snorkeling class going on at the same time, so Sophia ended up practicing in a basement storage room, where they were refurbishing the hotel's baby grand.

It was much harder to find pianos for Sophia in foreign

countries, and ingenuity was often required. London, of all places, proved surprisingly difficult. We were there for four days, because Jed was receiving an award for his book *The Interpretation of Murder,* a historical thriller based on Sigmund Freud's one and only visit to the United States in 1909. Jed's book was the #1 best seller in the UK for a while, and he was treated as something of a celebrity. This didn't help me one bit on the music front. When I asked the concierge at our boutique Chelsea hotel (courtesy of Jed's publisher) if we might find a time to practice on the piano in their library, she looked horrified, as if I'd asked to turn the hotel into a Laotian refugee camp.

"The *library*? Oh my goodness, no. I'm afraid not."

Later that day, a maid evidently reported to her superiors that Lulu was practicing violin in our room, and she was asked to stop. Fortunately, through the Internet I found a place in London that rented piano practice rooms for a small hourly fee. Every day, while Jed was doing his radio and television interviews, the girls and I would march out of the hotel and take a bus to the store, which resembled a funeral parlor and was squeezed between two falafel shops. After ninety minutes of practicing, we'd take a bus back to the hotel.

We did this kind of thing all over the place. In Leuven, Belgium, we practiced in a former convent. In another city, which I no longer recall, I found a Spanish restaurant with a piano that allowed Sophia to practice between 3:00 P.M. and 5:00 P.M., while the staff mopped the floor and set the tables for dinner. Occasionally, Jed got annoyed at me for making our vacations tense. "So, shall we see the Colosseum this afternoon," he'd say sardonically, "or go to that piano store again?"

Sophia got mad at me too. She hated it when I told hotel

people she was a "concert pianist." "Don't say that, Mommy! It's not true and it's embarrassing."

I totally disagreed. "You're a pianist, and you give concerts, Sophia. That's makes you a concert pianist."

Finally, all too often, Lulu and I got into tedious, escalating arguments, wasting so much time we'd miss a museum's opening hours or have to cancel a dinner reservation.

It was worth it. Whenever we got back to New Haven, Sophia and Lulu always stunned their music teachers with the progress they'd made away from home. Shortly after a trip to Xi'an, China—where I made Sophia practice at the crack of dawn for two hours before I would allow us to go see the 8000 life-sized Terracotta Warriors commissioned by China's first emperor, Qin Shi Huang, to serve him in the afterlife—Sophia won her second concerto competition, this time playing Mozart's Concerto no. 15 in B-flat Major. Meanwhile, Lulu was invited to play as the first violinist in all kinds of trios and quartets, and we suddenly found ourselves being wooed by other violin teachers, who were always on the lookout for young talent.

But even I have to admit that it sometimes got hard. I remember once we took a vacation to Greece with my parents. After seeing Athens (where we managed to slip in a little practicing between the Acropolis and the Temple of Poseidon), we took a small plane to the island of Crete. We arrived at our bed-and-breakfast around three in the afternoon, and my father wanted to head out immediately. He couldn't wait to show the girls the Palace of Knossos, where according to legend the Minoan King Minos kept the Minotaur, a monster with a man's body and bull's head, imprisoned in an underground labyrinth.

"Okay, Dad," I said. "But Lulu and I just have ten minutes of violin to do first."

Everyone exchanged alarmed glances. "How about practicing after dinner?" my mother suggested.

"No, Mom," I said firmly. "Lulu promised she'd do this, because she wanted to stop early yesterday. But if she cooperates, it really should just take ten minutes. We'll go easy today."

I wouldn't wish the misery that followed on anyone: Jed, Sophia, Lulu, and I cooped up in one claustrophobic room, with Jed lying on top of the bedspread, grimly trying to focus on an old issue of the *International Herald Tribune;* Sophia hiding in the bathroom reading; my parents waiting in the lobby, afraid to interfere and afraid other guests would overhear Lulu and me bickering, yelling, and provoking each other. ("That note was flat again, Lulu." "Actually, it was sharp, Mommy, you don't know anything.") Obviously, I couldn't stop after ten minutes when Lulu had refused to play even a single scale properly. When it was all over, Lulu was furious and tear-stained, Jed was tight-lipped, my parents were sleepy—and the Palace of Knossos was closed for the day.

I don't know how my daughters will look back on all this twenty years from now. Will they tell their own children, "My mother was a controlling fanatic who even in India made us practice before we could see Bombay and New Delhi"? Or will they have softer memories? Perhaps Lulu will recall playing the first movement of the Bruch Violin Concerto beautifully in Agra, in front of an arched hotel window that looked straight out to the Taj Mahal; we didn't fight that day for some reason—probably jet lag. Will Sophia recall with bitterness the time I laid into her at a piano in Barcelona because her fingers were not kicking high enough? If so, I hope she also remembers Rocque-brune, a village perched on a cliff in France, where the manager of our hotel heard Sophia practicing and invited her to perform for the entire restaurant that evening. In a glass-windowed room overlooking the Mediterranean, Sophia played Mendelssohn's Rondo Capriccioso, and got bravos and hugs from all the guests.

15

Popo

Florence

In January 2006, my mother-in-law, Florence, called from her apartment in Manhattan. "I just got a call from the doctor's office," she said in an odd, slightly exasperated voice, "and now they're telling me that I have acute *leukemia*." Just two months earlier, Florence had been diagnosed with early-stage breast cancer, but true to her indomitable personality, she'd gone through surgery and radiation without a complaint. The last I'd heard, everything was fine, and she was back on the New York art scene, thinking about writing a second book.

My stomach tightened. Florence looked sixty but was about to turn seventy-five. "That can't be right, Florence, it must be a mistake," I said aloud, stupidly. "Let me get Jed on the phone, and he'll figure out what's going on. Don't worry. Everything will be all right."

Everything wasn't all right. A week after our conversation, Florence had checked into New York Presbyterian Hospital and was starting chemotherapy. After hours of agonizing research and third and fourth opinions, Jed had helped Florence choose a less harsh arsenic-based treatment plan that wouldn't make her as sick. Florence always listened to Jed. As she liked to tell Sophia and Lulu, she had adored him from the moment he was born, one month premature. "He was jaundiced and all yellow and looked like a wrinkled old man," she used to laugh. "But I thought he was perfect." Jed and Florence had a lot in common. He shared his mother's aesthetic sensibilities and eye for good proportions. Everyone said he was her spitting image, and that was always meant as a compliment.

My mother-in-law was gorgeous when she was young. In her college yearbook, she looks like Rita Hayworth. Even at fifty, which is how old she was when I first met her, she turned heads at parties. She was also witty and charming, but definitely judgmental. You could always tell which outfits she found tacky, which dishes too rich, which people too eager. Once I came downstairs in a new suit, and Florence's face brightened. "You look terrific, Amy," she said warmly. "You're putting yourself together so much better these days."

Florence was an unusual combination. She was fascinated by grotesque objects and always said that "pretty" things bored her. She had an amazing eye, and had made some money in the 1970s by investing in works by relatively unknown modern artists. These artists—among them Robert Arneson and Sam Gilliam—all eventually got discovered, and Florence's purchases skyrocketed in value. Florence never envied anyone, and could be strangely insensitive to people who envied her. She didn't mind being alone; she prized her independence and had turned down offers of second marriage from many rich and successful men. Although she liked stylish clothes and art gallery openings, her favorite things in the world were swimming in Crystal Lake (where she had spent every summer as a child), making dinner for old friends, and most of all, being with her granddaughters Sophia and Lulu, who, at Florence's request, had always called her "Popo."

Florence made it into remission by March, after six weeks of chemotherapy. By then, she was a frail shadow of herself—I remember how small she looked against the white hospital pillows, like a 75% photocopy reduction of herself—but she still had all her hair, a decent appetite, and the same buoyant personality. She was ecstatic about being discharged.

Jed and I knew the remission was only temporary. The doctors had repeatedly warned us that Florence's prognosis was poor. Her leukemia was aggressive and would almost certainly relapse within six months to a year. Because of her age, there was no possibility of a bone marrow transplant—in short, no possibility of a cure. But Florence didn't understand her disease and had no idea how hopeless things were. Jed tried a few times to explain the situation, but Florence was always stubbornly obtuse and upbeat, and nothing seemed to sink in. "Oh, dear—I'm going to have to spend a lot of time at the gym when this is all over," she'd say surreally. "My muscle tone's all gone."

In the immediate term, we had to decide what to do with Florence. Living on her own was out of the question: She was too weak to walk and needed frequent blood transfusions. And she really didn't have much family she could turn to. By her choice she had almost no contact with her ex-husband, Sy, and her daughter lived much farther away.

I proposed what seemed the obvious solution: Florence would come live with us in New Haven. My mother's elderly parents lived with us in Indiana when I was little. My father's mother lived with my uncle in Chicago until she died at the age of eighty-seven. I've always assumed that I would take in my parents if the need arose. This is the Chinese way.

To my astonishment, Jed was reluctant. There was no question of his devotion to Florence. But he reminded me that I had often had trouble with Florence and gotten angry at her; that she and I had wildly different views about child-rearing; that we both had strong personalities; and that, even ill, Florence was unlikely to keep her views to herself. He asked me to imagine what it would be like if Lulu and I got into one of our raging, thrashing fights and Florence felt the need to intervene on behalf of her granddaughter.

Jed was right of course. Florence and I got along great for years—she introduced me to the world of modern art, and I used to love accompanying her to museum and gallery events—but we started having conflicts after Sophia was born. In fact, it was through butting heads with Florence that I first became aware of some of the deep differences between Chinese and (at least one variant of) Western parenting. Above all, Florence had taste. She was a connoisseur of art, food, and wine. She liked luxurious fabrics and dark chocolate. Whenever we returned from travels, she always asked the girls about the colors and smells they'd encountered. Another thing Florence had definite taste about was childhood. She believed that childhood should be full of spontaneity, freedom, discovery, and experience.

At Crystal Lake, Florence felt that her granddaughters should be able to swim, walk, and explore wherever they pleased. By contrast, I told them that if they stepped off our front porch, kidnappers would get them. I also told them that the deep parts of the lake had ferocious biting fish. I may have gone overboard, but sometimes being carefree means being careless. Once when Florence was babysitting for us at the lake, I came home to find two-year-old Sophia running around outside by herself with a pair of garden shears as large was she was. I snatched them furiously away. "She was going to cut some wildflowers," Florence said wistfully.

The truth is I'm not good at enjoying life. It's not one of my strengths. I keep a lot of to-do lists and hate massages and Caribbean vacations. Florence saw childhood as something fleeting to be enjoyed. I saw childhood as a training period, a time to build character and invest for the future. Florence always wanted just one full day to spend with each girl—she begged me for that. But I never had a full day for them to spare. The girls barely had time as it was to do their homework, speak Chinese with their tutor, and practice their instruments.

Florence liked rebelliousness and moral dilemmas. She also liked psychological complexity. I did too, but not when it was applied to my kids. "Sophia is *so envious* of her new sister," Florence once giggled, shortly after Lulu was born. "She just wants to ship Lulu back where she came from."

"No, she doesn't," I snapped. "Sophia loves her new sister." I felt that Florence was generating sibling rivalry by looking for it. There are all kinds of psychological disorders in the West that don't exist in Asia.

Being Chinese, I almost never had any open confrontations with Florence. When I said "butting heads with Florence" earlier, what I meant was criticizing and railing against her to Jed behind her back. With Florence I was always accommodating and hypocritically good-natured about her many suggestions. So Jed had a point, especially since he'd borne the brunt of the conflict.

But none of that mattered one bit, because Florence was Jed's mother. For Chinese people, when it comes to parents, nothing is negotiable. Your parents are your parents, you owe everything to them (even if you don't), and you have to do everything for them (even if it destroys your life).

In early April, Jed checked Florence out of the hospital and brought her to New Haven, where he carried her up to our second floor. Florence was incredibly excited and happy, as if we were all at a resort together. She stayed in our guest room, next to the girls' bedroom and just down the hall from our master bedroom. We hired a nurse to cook and care for her, and physical therapists were always coming and going. Almost every night, Jed, the girls, and I had dinner with Florence; for the first couple of weeks, it was always in her room because she couldn't come downstairs. Once, I invited a few of her friends and threw a wine and cheese party in her room. When Florence saw the cheeses I'd picked, she was aghast and sent me out for different ones. Instead of being mad, I was glad that she was still Florence and that good taste ran in my daughters' genes. I also made a note of which cheeses never to buy again.

Although there were constant scares—Jed had to race Florence to the New Haven hospital at least twice a week—Florence seemed to recover miraculously in our house. She had an enormous appetite and gained weight rapidly. On her birthday, May 3, we were able to all go out to a nice restaurant. Our friends Henry and Marina came with us and couldn't believe this was the same Florence they'd seen in the hospital six weeks earlier. In a high-necked asymmetrical Issey Miyake jacket, she was glamorous again and didn't even look sick.

Just a few days later, on May 7, Sophia had her Bat Mitzvah at our house. Earlier that same morning we'd had another crisis, with Jed rushing Florence to the hospital for an emergency blood transfusion. But they made it back on time, and Florence looked fabulous when the eighty guests arrived. After the ceremony, under a perfect blue sky, on tables with white tulips, we served French toast, strawberries, and dim sum—Sophia and Popo had planned the menu—and Jed and I marveled at how much you have to spend to keep things simple and unpretentious.

A week later, Florence decided that she was well enough to go back to her own New York apartment, as long as the nurse went with her. She died in her apartment on May 21, apparently from a stroke that killed her instantly. She had plans to go out for drinks that evening and never knew that her time was limited.

At the funeral, both Sophia and Lulu read short speeches they'd written themselves. Here's part of what Lulu said:

> When Popo was living at my family's house over the last month, I spent a lot of time with her, whether it was eating lunch together, playing cards with her, or just talking. On two nights, we were left alone together—"babysitting" each other. Even though she was sick and couldn't walk well, she made me feel not scared at all. She was a very strong person. When I think of Popo, I think of her happy and laughing. She loved to be happy and that made me feel happy too. I'm really going to miss Popo a lot.

And here's part of what Sophia said:

> Popo always wanted intellectual stimulation, full happiness—to get the utmost vitality and thought out of every minute. And I think she got it, right up to the end. I hope someday I can learn to do the same.

When I heard Sophia and Lulu say these words, several things came to mind. I was proud and glad that Jed and I had taken Florence in, the Chinese way, and that the girls had witnessed us doing it. I was also proud and glad that Sophia and Lulu had helped take care of Florence. But with the words "loved to be happy" and "full happiness" ringing in my head, I also wondered whether down the road if I were sick, the girls would take me into their homes and do the same for me—or whether they would opt for happiness and freedom.

Happiness is not a concept I tend to dwell on. Chinese parenting does not address happiness. This has always worried me. When I see the piano- and violin-induced calluses on my daughters' fingertips, or the teeth marks on the piano, I'm sometimes seized with doubt.

But here's the thing. When I look around at all the Western families that fall apart—all the grown sons and daughters who can't stand to be around their parents or don't even talk to them—I have a hard time believing that Western parenting does a better job with happiness. It's amazing how many older Western parents I've met who've said, shaking their heads sadly, "As a parent you just can't win. No matter what you do, your kids will grow up resenting you."

By contrast, I can't tell you how many Asian kids I've met who, while acknowledging how oppressively strict and brutally demanding their parents were, happily describe themselves as devoted to their parents and unbelievably grateful to them, seemingly without a trace of bitterness or resentment.

I'm really not sure why this is. Maybe it's brainwashing. Or maybe it's Stockholm syndrome. But here's one thing I'm sure of: Western children are definitely no happier than Chinese ones.

16

The Birthday Card

Everyone was moved by what Sophia and Lulu said at Florence's funeral. "If only Florence could have heard them," Florence's best friend Sylvia said sadly afterward. "Nothing would have made her happier." How, other friends asked, could a thirteen- and ten-year-old capture Florence so perfectly?

But there's a backstory.

It actually starts years earlier, when the girls were quite young, maybe seven and four. It was my birthday, and we were celebrating at a mediocre Italian restaurant, because Jed had forgotten to make reservations at a better place.

Obviously feeling guilty, Jed was trying to act jaunty. "O-k-a-y! This is going to be a g-r-e-a-t birthday dinner for Mommy! Right, girls? And you each have a little surprise for Mommy— right, girls?"

I was soaking some stale focaccia in the small dish of olive oil the server had given us. At Jed's urging, Lulu handed me her "surprise," which turned out to be a card. More accurately, it was a piece of paper folded crookedly in half, with a big happy face on the front. Inside, "Happy Birthday, Mommy! Love, Lulu" was scrawled in crayon above another happy face. The card couldn't have taken Lulu more than twenty seconds to make.

I know just what Jed would have done. He would have said, "Oh, how nice—thank you, honey," and planted a stiff kiss on Lulu's forehead. Then he probably would have said that he wasn't very hungry, and was only going to have a bowl of soup, or on second thought just bread and water, but the rest of us could order as much as we goddamn liked.

I gave the card back to Lulu. "I don't want this," I said. "I want a better one—one that you've put some thought and effort into. I have a special box, where I keep all my cards from you and Sophia, and this one can't go in there."

"What?" said Lulu in disbelief. I saw beads of sweat start to form on Jed's forehead.

I grabbed the card again and flipped it over. I pulled out a pen from my purse and scrawled "Happy Birthday Lulu Whoopee!" I added a big sour face. "What if I gave you this for your birthday, Lulu—would you like that? But I would never do that, Lulu. No—I get you magicians and giant slides that cost me hundreds of dollars. I get you huge ice cream cakes shaped like penguins, and I spend half my salary on stupid sticker and eraser party favors that everyone just throws away. I work so hard to give you good birthdays! I deserve better than this. So I *reject* this." I threw the card back.

"May I please be excused for a second?" Sophia asked in a small voice. "I need to do something."

"Let me see it, Sophia. Hand it over."

Eyes wide with terror, Sophia slowly pulled out her own card. It was bigger than Lulu's, made of red construction paper, but while more effusive, equally empty. She had drawn a few flowers and written "I love you! Happy Birthday to the Best Mommy in the World! #1 Mommy!"

"That's nice, Sophia," I said coldly, "but not good enough either. When I was your age, I wrote poems for my mother on her birthday. I got up early and cleaned the house and made her breakfast. I tried to think of creative ideas and made her coupons that said things like 'One Free Car Wash.'"

"I wanted to make something better, but you said I had to play piano," Sophia protested indignantly.

"You should have gotten up earlier," I responded.

Later that night, I received two much better birthday cards, which I loved and still have.

I recounted this story to Florence shortly afterward. She laughed in astonishment, but to my surprise, she was not disapproving. "Maybe I should have tried something similar with my kids," she said thoughtfully. "It just always seemed that if you had to *ask* for something, it wouldn't be worth anything."

"I think it's too idealistic to expect children to do the right things on their own," I said. "Also, if you force them to do what you want, you don't have to be mad at them."

"But they'll be mad at you," Florence pointed out.

I thought of this exchange many years later, the day of the funeral. According to Jewish law, burials must take place as soon as possible after death, ideally within twenty-four hours. The suddenness of Florence's death was unexpected, and in one day Jed had to arrange for a plot, a rabbi, a funeral home, and the service. As always, Jed handled everything quickly and efficiently, keeping his emotions to himself, but I could tell that his whole body was shaking, his grief too much to bear.

I found the girls in their bedroom that morning, huddled together. They both looked stunned and frightened. No one so close to them had ever died before. They had never attended a funeral. And Popo had just been laughing in the next room a week earlier.

I told the girls that they each had to write a short speech about Popo, which they would read at the service that afternoon.

"No, please, Mommy, don't make me," Sophia said tearfully. "I really don't feel like it."

"I can't," Lulu sobbed. "Go away."

"You *have* to," I ordered. "Both of you. Popo would have wanted it."

Sophia's first draft was terrible, rambling and superficial. Lulu's wasn't so great either, but I held my elder daughter to a higher standard. Perhaps because I was so upset myself, I lashed out at her. "How *could* you, Sophia?" I said viciously. "This is awful. It has no insight. It has no depth. It's like a Hallmark card—which Popo hated. You are so selfish. Popo loved you so much—and you—produce—*this!*"

Crying uncontrollably, Sophia shouted back at me, which startled me because like Jed—unlike Lulu and me—Sophia's anger usually simmers, rarely boiling over. "You have no right to say what Popo would have wanted! You didn't even like

Popo—you have this fixation with Chinese values and respect for elders, but all you did was mock her. Every little thing she did—even *making couscous*—reflected some terrible moral deficiency for you. Why are you so—Manichaean? Why does everything have to be black or white?"

I didn't mock her, I thought to myself indignantly. I was just protecting my daughters from a romanticized model of child-rearing doomed to failure. Besides, I was the one who invited Florence to everything, who made sure she saw her granddaughters all the time. I gave Florence her greatest source of happiness—beautiful, respectful, accomplished grandchildren she could be proud of. How could Sophia, who was so smart and even knew the word *Manichaean,* not see that and attack me instead?

Externally, I ignored Sophia's outburst. Instead, I offered some editorial suggestions—things about her grandmother that she might mention. I asked her to talk about Crystal Lake and going to museums with Florence.

Sophia took none of my suggestions. Slamming the door after I left, she locked herself in her bedroom and rewrote the speech herself. She refused to show it to me, wouldn't look at me, even after she had cooled down and changed into a black dress and black tights. And later, at the service when Sophia was at the podium speaking, looking dignified and calm, I didn't miss the pointed lines:

> Popo never settled for anything—a dishonest conversation, a film not quite true to the book, a slightly false display of emotion. Popo wouldn't allow people to put words in my mouth.

It was a wonderful speech. Lulu's was too; she had spoken with great perceptiveness and poise for a ten-year-old. I could just imagine a beaming Florence saying, "I'm bursting."

On the other hand, Florence was right. The kids were definitely mad at me. But as a Chinese mother, I put that out of my head.

17

Caravan to Chautauqua

The summer after Florence's passing was a difficult one. To begin with, I ran over Sophia's foot. She jumped out of my car to grab a tennis racket while I was still backing up, and her left ankle got caught in the front wheel. Sophia and I both fainted. She ended up having surgery under full anesthesia and two big screws put in. Then she had to wear a huge boot and use crutches for the rest of the summer, which put her in a bad mood but at least gave her a lot of time to practice the piano.

One good thing in our lives, though, was Coco, who got cuter by the day. She had the same strange effect on all four of us: Just looking at her lifted our spirits. This was true even though all my ambitions for her had been replaced by a single dynamic: She would look at me with her pleading chocolate almond eyes— and I would do whatever she wanted, which was usually to go running for four miles, rain, sleet, or shine. In return, Coco was compassionate. I knew she hated it when I yelled at the girls, but she never judged me and knew that I was trying to be a good mother.

It didn't upset me that I had revised my dreams for Coco—I just wanted her to be happy. I had finally come to see that Coco was an animal, with intrinsically far less potential than Sophia and Lulu. Although it is true that some dogs are on bomb squads or drug-sniffing teams, it is perfectly fine for most dogs not to have a profession or even any special skills.

Around that time, I had a life-changing conversation with my brilliant friend and colleague Peter, who speaks six languages and reads eleven, including Sanskrit and Ancient Greek. A gifted pianist who had debuted in New York as a teenager, Peter attended one of Sophia's recitals at the Neighborhood Music School.

Afterward, Peter told me that he thought Sophia's playing was really extraordinary. Then he added, "I don't want to meddle or anything, but have you thought about the Yale School of Music? Maybe Sophia should audition for one of the piano faculty there."

"You mean . . . change teachers?" I said, my mind racing. The Neighborhood Music School had been one of my favorite places for almost a decade.

"Well, yes," said Peter. "I'm sure the Neighborhood Music School is a wonderful place. But compared to the other kids here Sophia's in a different league. Of course it all depends on what your goals are. Maybe you just want to keep things fun."

This took me aback. No one had ever accused me of trying to keep things fun. And coincidentally, I'd just received a phone call from another friend raising the very same question about Lulu.

That night, I sent two crucial e-mails. The first was to a violinist and recent graduate of the Yale School of Music named Kiwon Nahm, whom I'd hired on occasion to help Lulu practice. The second was to Professor Wei-Yi Yang, the most recent addition to Yale's illustrious piano faculty and by all accounts a piano prodigy and sensation.

Things moved faster than I expected. By a tremendous stroke of luck, Professor Yang knew of Sophia; he had heard her play a Mozart piano quartet at a fund-raiser and been favorably impressed. He and I agreed to meet for lunch in late August, when he returned from his summer concertizing.

Something equally exciting happened with Lulu. Kiwon—who had debuted at Lincoln Center as a soloist at the age of twelve—generously mentioned Lulu to a former teacher named Almita Vamos. Mrs. Vamos and her husband, Roland, are among the leading violin instructors in the world. They've been honored by the White House six times. Their former students include well-known soloists like Rachel Barton and many winners of prestigious international competitions. Based in Chicago, they teach only very gifted students, a large proportion of them Asian.

We waited on tenterhooks to see if Mrs. Vamos would respond. A week later, the e-mail came. Mrs. Vamos invited Lulu to come play for her at the Chautauqua Institution in upstate New York, where she was in residence that summer. The date Mrs. Vamos chose was July 29—only three weeks away.

For the next twenty days, Lulu did nothing but practice violin. To squeeze as much improvement out of Lulu as possible, I paid Kiwon to come twice, sometimes three times a day to work with her. When Jed saw the cashed checks, he couldn't believe his eyes. I told him we'd make up for it by not going out to dinner all summer and not buying new clothes. "Also," I said hopefully, "there is the advance you just got for your novel."

"I'd better start on a sequel now," Jed replied grimly.

"There is nothing better to spend our money on than our children," I said.

Jed was in for another unpleasant surprise. I had imagined that the drive to see Mrs. Vamos would take three, maybe four hours, and had told Jed as much. The day before we were scheduled to leave, Jed got on MapQuest and said, "So where's this place again?"

Unfortunately, I hadn't realized that New York State is so big. Chautauqua turned out to be located near Lake Erie, not far from Canada.

"Amy, it's nine hours away—not three," Jed said in exasperation. "How long are we staying?"

"Just one night. I signed Sophia up for a computer animation course, which starts Monday—something exciting for her while she's on crutches. But I'm sure we can make the drive in seven—"

"What are we supposed to do with Coco?" Jed interrupted. Coco had been housebroken for only two months and had never traveled anywhere before.

"I thought it would be fun to take her with us. It'll be our first vacation together," I said.

"It's not exactly a vacation to drive eighteen hours in two days," Jed pointed out, a little selfishly, I thought. "And what about Sophia's broken foot? Isn't she supposed to keep her leg elevated? How are we going to fit everybody in the car?"

We drove an old Jeep Cherokee. I suggested that Sophia could lie down in the backseat with her head on Lulu's lap and her leg propped up on pillows. Coco could go all the way in back with the suitcases and violins (yes, plural, which I'll explain). "There's one more thing," I added. "I asked Kiwon if she would come with us and told her that I'd pay her by the hour, including transportation time."

"What?" Jed was incredulous. "That's going to cost three thousand dollars. And how are we going to fit her in the car? Put her in the back with Coco?"

"She can take her own car—I told her I'd pay for gas—but actually she really didn't want to make the trip. It's a long way, and she'd have to cancel her other teaching hours. To make it more appealing for her, I invited her new boyfriend, Aaron, to come too, and offered to put them up for three nights at a nice hotel. I found an amazing place called the William Seward Inn, and I booked them each a double deluxe room."

"For three nights," said Jed. "You're joking."

"If you want, you and I can stay at a cheaper place, to save money."

"I don't want."

"Aaron's a great guy," I told Jed persuasively. "You're going to love him. He's a French horn player, and he loves dogs. He's offered to watch Coco for free while we're with Mrs. Vamos."

We left at the crack of dawn, with Kiwon and Aaron in a white Honda following behind our white Jeep. It wasn't a pleasant trip. Jed insisted on driving the whole way, a macho thing, which gets on my nerves. Sophia insisted that she was in pain and losing circulation. "Remind me again—why am I coming on this trip?" she asked innocently.

"Because the family always has to stay together," I replied.

"Also, this is an important event for Lulu, and you have to support your sister."

The whole nine hours I sat tense and cross-legged in the front passenger seat, with Coco's food, equipment, and fuzzy sleepy mat where my feet should have been. My head was wedged between Sophia's two horizontal crutches, which were suctioned in place on the windshield.

Meanwhile, Lulu was acting like she didn't have a care in the world. That's how I knew she was terrified.

18

The Swimming Hole

"What?" Jed asked. "Tell me you didn't say what I think you said." This was a month before our trip to Chautauqua.

"I said I'm thinking about cashing in my pension funds. Not all of them; just the ones from Cleary." Cleary, Gottlieb, Steen, and Hamilton was the name of the Wall Street law firm where I'd worked before Sophia was born.

"That makes absolutely no sense from any point of view," Jed said. "First, you'd have to pay a huge tax and forfeit half the amount. More important, we need to save that money for our retirement. That's what pension funds are for. It's part of progress and civilization."

"There's something I need to buy," I said.

"What is it, Amy?" Jed asked. "If there's something you really want, I'll find a way for us to get it."

I got so lucky in love. Jed is handsome, funny, smart, *and* he tolerates my bad taste and tendency to get ripped off. I actually don't buy that many things. I don't enjoy shopping, I don't get facials or manicures, and I don't buy jewelry. But every once in a while there will be something that I get an uncontrollable urge to own—a 1500-pound clay horse from China, for example, which disintegrated the following winter—and Jed has always managed to get it for me. In this case, I was overcome with a powerful urge to buy a really good violin for Lulu.

I contacted some reputable violin dealers who had been recommended to me, two in New York, one in Boston, one in Philadelphia. I asked each dealer to send me three violins for Lulu to try, within a certain price range. They always sent me four violins, three in the price range specified, and one that "is a little out of your price range"—meaning twice as expensive—"but that I decided to send along anyway because it's an extraordinary instrument and might be just what you're looking for." Violin shops are similar to rug merchants in Uzbekistan in this way. As we hit each new price plateau, I tried to convince Jed that a fine violin was an investment, like artwork or real estate. "So we're actually making money the more we spend?" he would reply drily.

Meanwhile, Lulu and I had a blast. Every time a big new box arrived by UPS, we couldn't wait to rip it open. It was fun playing on the different violins, comparing the wood and their different tones, reading about their difference provenances, trying to glean their different personalities. We tried a few new but mainly older violins, from the 1930s or earlier. We tried violins from England, France, and Germany, but mostly from Italy, usually Cremona, Genoa, or Naples. Lulu and I would get the whole family to do blindfold tests, to see if we could tell which violin was which and whether our preferences stayed the same if we couldn't see the violins.

The thing about Lulu and me is that we're at once incompatible and really close. We can have a great time but also hurt each other deeply. We always know what the other is thinking—which form of psychological torture is being deployed—and we both can't help ourselves. We both tend to explode and then feel fine. Jed has never understood how one minute Lulu and I will be screaming death threats at each other, and the next minute we'll be lying in bed, Lulu's arms wrapped around me, talking about violins or reading and laughing together.

Anyway, when we finally arrived at Mrs. Vamos's studio at the Chautauqua Institution, we had with us not one but three violins. We hadn't been able to make a final decision.

"Wonderful!" said Mrs. Vamos. "How fun. I love trying violins." Mrs. Vamos was down-to-earth and as sharp as a tack, with a quirky sense of humor. She was opinionated ("I hate Viotti 23. Boring!") and exuded power and impressiveness. She was also amazing with kids—or at least with Lulu, whom she seemed to take to instantly. Mrs. Vamos and Jed hit it off too. The only person I don't think Mrs. Vamos liked very much was me. I got the feeling that she had encountered hundreds, possibly thousands, of Asian mothers and that she found me unaesthetic.

Lulu played the first movement of Mozart's Concerto no. 3 for Mrs. Vamos. Afterward, Mrs. Vamos told Lulu that she was extremely musical. She asked Lulu if she liked playing the violin. I held my breath, honestly not sure what the answer would be. Lulu replied yes. Mrs. Vamos then told Lulu that while she had the advantage of being naturally musical—something that couldn't be taught—she lagged behind in technique. She asked Lulu if she practiced scales ("Sort of") and études ("What are those?").

Mrs. Vamos told Lulu that all this had to change if she really wanted to be a good violinist. She needed to do tons of scales and études to develop impeccable technique, muscle memory, and perfect intonation. Mrs. Vamos also told Lulu that she was moving much too slowly; it wasn't good enough to spend six months on one movement of a concerto. "My students your age can learn an *entire concerto* in two weeks—you should be able to do that too."

Mrs. Vamos then worked with Lulu on the Mozart line by line, transforming Lulu's playing right before my eyes. She was an exceptional teacher: demanding but fun, critical but inspiring. When an hour was up—by then five or six students had come in and were sitting with their instruments on the floor—Mrs. Vamos gave Lulu some things to work on by herself and told us that she'd be happy to see her again the next day.

I couldn't believe it. Mrs. Vamos wanted to see Lulu again. I almost leaped out of my chair—and probably would have if at that moment I hadn't seen Coco fly by our window followed by Aaron on the leash behind her.

"What was that?" asked Mrs. Vamos.

"It's our dog, Coco," explained Lulu.

"I love dogs. And yours looks really cute," said one of the most famous violin teachers in the world. "We can see how those violins sound tomorrow too," she added. "I like the Italian, but maybe the French one will open up."

Back at the hotel, I was trembling with excitement. I couldn't wait to start practicing—what an opportunity! I knew that Mrs. Vamos was surrounded by driven Asians, but I was all the more determined to astonish her, to show her what we were made of.

I pulled out the Mozart score, just in time to see Lulu sink into a comfortable armchair. "Ah-h-h," she sighed contentedly, leaning her head back. "That was a good day. Let's have dinner."

"Dinner?" I couldn't believe my ears. "Lulu, Mrs. Vamos gave you an *assignment*. She wants to see how *fast* you can improve. This is hugely important—it's not a game. Come on. Let's start."

"What are you talking about, Mommy? I've been playing violin for *five hours*." This was true: she had practiced all morning with Kiwon before going to see Mrs. Vamos. "I need a break. I can't play more now. Plus it's five-thirty already. It's dinnertime."

"Five-thirty is not dinnertime. We'll practice first, then reward ourselves with dinner. I've already made reservations at an Italian restaurant—your favorite."

"Oh-h, no-o-o," Lulu moaned. "Are you serious? What time?"

"What time what?"

"What time is the dinner reservation?"

"Oh! Nine o'clock," I replied, then regretted it.

"NINE? *NINE?* That's crazy, Ma! I refuse. I refuse!"

"Lulu, I'll change it to—"

"I REFUSE! I can't practice now. I won't!"

I won't get into the details of what ensued. Two facts should suffice. One, we didn't have dinner until nine. Two, we didn't practice. In retrospect, I don't know where I got the strength and temerity to fight Lulu. Just the memory of that evening makes me feel exhausted.

But the next morning, Lulu got up and on her own went to practice with Kiwon, so all was not lost. Jed suggested in the strongest terms that I go for a long run with Coco far, far away, which I did. At noon we went back to Mrs. Vamos, Kiwon accompanying us, and the session again went very well.

I had harbored hopes that Mrs. Vamos might say, "I'd love to take Lulu on as my student. Is there any chance of your flying out to Chicago for lessons once a month?" To which I would have said yes, absolutely. But instead Mrs. Vamos suggested that Lulu work intensively with Kiwon as her teacher for the next year. "You won't find anyone with better technique than Kiwon," Mrs. Vamos said, smiling at her former student, "and Lulu, you have a lot of catching up to do. But in a year or so, you might think about auditioning for the Pre-College program at Juilliard. Kiwon, you did that, right? It's extremely competitive, but if you work really hard, Lulu, I bet you could get in. And of course, I hope you'll come back and see me next summer."

Before getting on the road for New Haven, Jed, the girls, and I drove to a nature reserve and found a beautiful swimming hole surrounded by beech trees and small waterfalls, which our innkeeper had said was one of the hidden gems of the area. Coco was afraid of going into the water—she'd never swum before—but Jed gently pulled her in to the deep center, where he let go of her. I was afraid Coco would drown, but just as Jed said she would, Coco dog-paddled safely back to shore while we clapped and cheered, toweling her off and giving her big hugs when she arrived.

That's one difference between a dog and a daughter, I thought to myself later. A dog can do something every dog can do—dog paddle, for example—and we applaud with pride and joy. Imagine how much easier it would be if we could do the same with daughters! But we can't; that would be negligence.

I had to keep my eye on the ball. Mrs. Vamos's message was crystal clear. It was time to get serious.

19

How You Get

to Carnegie Hall

Sophia and her taskmaster (with my father watching)

My heart sank. The score looked disappointingly sparse, a few staccato notes here and there, not a lot of density or vertical range. And such a short piece: six scruffy xeroxed pages.

Sophia and I were in Professor Wei-Yi Yang's piano studio at the Yale School of Music. It was a large rectangular room with two black Steinway baby grand pianos standing side by side, one for the teacher, one for the student. I was staring at "Juliet as a Young Girl" from Sergei Prokofiev's *Romeo and Juliet,* which Wei-Yi had just proposed that Sophia play for an international piano competition that was coming up.

When Wei-Yi and I first met, he explained that he'd never had a student as young as Sophia, who was barely fourteen. He taught only Yale piano graduate students and a few Yale undergraduates of unusual caliber. But having heard Sophia play, he was willing to take her on with one condition: that she didn't require any special treatment because of her age. I assured him that this would be no problem.

I love being able to count on Sophia. She has wells of inner strength. Even more than me, she can take anything: exclusion, excoriation, humiliation, loneliness.

Thus began Sophia's baptism of fire. Like Mrs. Vamos, Wei-Yi had expectations that were of an order galactically beyond what we'd been used to. The stack of music he handed Sophia at her first lesson—six Bach inventions, a book of Moszkowski études, a Beethoven sonata, a toccata by Khachaturian, and Brahms's Rhapsody in G Minor—stunned even me. Sophia had some catching up to do, he explained; her technical foundation was not what it should be, and there were some gaping holes in her repertoire. Even more intimidating was when he said to Sophia, "And don't waste my time with wrong notes. At your level, there's no excuse. It's your job to get the notes right, so we can work on other things during the lesson."

But two months later, when Wei-Yi Yang proposed the pieces from the suite *Romeo and Juliet,* I had the opposite reaction. The

Prokofiev didn't look demanding all—it didn't strike me as a competition winner. And why Prokofiev? The only thing I knew about Prokofiev was *Peter and the Wolf*. Why not something hard, like Rachmaninov?

"Oh, this piece," I said aloud. "Sophia's old piano teacher thought it was too easy for her." This wasn't entirely true. Actually, it wasn't even a little true. But I didn't want Wei-Yi to think I was challenging his judgment.

"Easy?" Wei-Yi boomed contemptuously. He had a deep baritone voice, which was strangely inconsonant with his slight, boyish frame. He was in his thirties, of mixed Chinese and Japanese descent, but raised in London and Russian-taught. "Prokofiev's piano concertos hold up the sky. And there is nothing—not one note—that is easy about this piece. I challenge anyone to play it well."

I liked this. I like authority figures. I like *experts*. This is the opposite of Jed, who hates authority and believes that most "experts" are charlatans. More important, the Prokofiev wasn't easy! Hurray! Professor Wei-Yi Yang, an expert, said so.

My heart skipped a beat. The first-prize winners for this competition would perform as soloists at Carnegie Hall. Until now Sophia had competed only in local competitions. I had gone crazy when Sophia played as a soloist with the Farmington Valley (all volunteer) Symphony. To jump from there to an international competition was daunting enough, but a chance at *Carnegie Hall*—I could hardly stand to think about it.

Over the next few months, Sophia and I learned what it was like to take piano lessons from a master. Watching Professor Yang teach Sophia "Juliet as a Young Girl" was one of the most amazing and humbling experiences I've ever had. As he helped Sophia bring the piece to life, adding layer upon layer of nuance, all I could think was, This man is a genius. I am a barbarian. Prokofiev is a genius. I am a cretin. Wei-Yi and Prokofiev are great. I am a cannibal.

Going to lessons with Wei-Yi became my favorite thing; I looked forward to it all week. At every session I would religiously take notes, the scales falling from my eyes. Occasionally, I felt out of my league. What did he mean by triads and tritones, and making harmonic sense of the music, and why did Sophia seem to get it all so quickly? Other times, I picked up things that Sophia missed—I watched Wei-Yi's demonstrations like a hawk, sometimes drawing sketches in my notebook to capture them. Back home the two of us would work together in a new way, jointly trying to absorb and implement Wei-Yi's insights and instructions. I no longer had to yell at Sophia or fight with her about practicing. She was stimulated and intrigued; it was as if a new world were opening up for her, and for me too, as a junior partner.

The hardest part of the Prokofiev was the elusive Juliet theme that formed the backbone of the piece. Here's what Sophia later wrote in a school essay about "Conquering Juliet":

> I had just played the last notes of "Juliet as a Young Girl," and the basement studio was dead silent. Professor Yang stared at me. I stared at the rug. My mom was scribbling furiously in our piano notebook.
>
> I reviewed the piece in my head. Was it the scales, or the jumps? I had nailed them all. The dynamics, or the tempo? I had obeyed every crescendo and ritard. As far as I could

tell, my rendition had been flawless. So what was wrong with these people, and what more could they possibly want from me?

At last, Professor Yang spoke. "Sophia, what temperature is this piece?"

I was tongue-tied.

"It's a trick question. I'll make it easier. Consider the middle section. What color is it?"

I realized I had to give an answer. "Blue? Light blue?"

"And what temperature is light blue?"

That was easy. "Light blue is cool."

"Then let the phrase be cool."

What kind of instruction was that? The piano is a percussion instrument. Temperature isn't part of the equation. I could hear the haunting, delicate melody in my head. Think, Sophia! I knew this was Juliet's theme. But who was Juliet, and how was she "cool"? I remembered something Professor Yang had mentioned the week before: Juliet was fourteen years old, just like me. How would I act if a handsome older boy suddenly declared his undying love for me? Well, I thought to myself, she already knows she's desirable, but she's also flattered and embarrassed. She's fascinated by him, but she's also shy and afraid of looking overeager. This was a coolness I could comprehend. I took a deep breath and began.

Shockingly, Professor Yang was pleased. "Better. Now do it again, but this time let Juliet be in your hands, not your facial expressions. Here, like this——" He took my place on the piano bench to demonstrate.

I will never forget how he transformed the little melody.

It was Juliet just as I had envisioned her: alluring, vulnerable, a little blasé. The secret, I began to realize, was letting the hand reflect the character of the piece. Professor Yang's was cupped in the shape of a tent; he coaxed the sound from the keys. His fingers were sinewy and elegant, like ballerinas' legs.

"Now you," he ordered.

Unfortunately, Juliet was only half the piece. The next page brought a new character: lovesick, testosterone-fueled Romeo. He posed a completely different challenge; his tone was as rich and muscular as Juliet's was ethereal and slender. And of course, Professor Yang had more questions for me to grapple with.

"Sophia, your Romeo and Juliet sound the same. What instruments are they played by?"

I didn't get it. Uh, piano? I thought to myself.

Professor Yang continued. "Sophia, this ballet was written for an entire orchestra. As a pianist, you must reproduce the sound of every instrument. So what is Juliet, and what is Romeo?"

Bewildered, I fingered the first few bars of each theme. "Juliet is . . . flute, maybe, and Romeo is . . . cello?"

As it turned out, Juliet was a bassoon. I was right about Romeo, though. In Prokofiev's original arrangement, his theme really is played by the cello. Romeo's character was always easier for me to understand. I'm not sure why; it definitely wasn't real-life inspiration. Maybe I just felt bad for him. Obviously he was doomed, and he was so hopelessly be-

sotted with Juliet. The slightest hint of her theme had him begging on his knees.

Whereas Juliet eluded me for a long time, I always knew I could get Romeo. His moodiness required a number of different playing techniques. At times he was sonorous and confident. Then, just a few measures later, he was desperate and pleading. I tried to train my hands like Professor Yang said. It was hard enough being both a soprano and a prima ballerina for Juliet; now I had to play the piano like a cellist.

I'll save the conclusion of Sophia's school essay for a later chapter.

The competition Sophia was preparing for was open to young pianists from all over the world, anyone who was not already a professional musician. Somewhat unusually, there was no live audition component. The winners would be chosen solely on the basis of a fifteen-minute unedited CD containing any piano repertoire of our choosing. Wei-Yi was emphatic about our CD opening with Sophia playing "Juliet as a Young Girl" followed immediately by "The Street Awakens," another short piece from *Romeo and Juliet*. Like the curator of an art exhibition, he carefully chose the other works—a Liszt Hungarian Rhapsody, a middle-period Beethoven sonata—that would complete the CD.

After eight grueling weeks, Wei-Yi said Sophia was ready. Late one Tuesday evening, after she had finished her homework and practicing, we drove to the studio of a professional audio engineer named Istvan to record Sophia's CD. The experience was traumatizing. At first, I didn't get it. This should be easy, I thought to myself. We can redo it as many times as it takes to get a perfect version. Totally wrong. What I didn't understand was (1) pianists' hands get tired; (2) it's extremely hard to play musically when there's no audience and you know every note is being recorded; and (3) as Sophia tearfully explained to me, the more she played and replayed her pieces, trying her hardest each time to pour emotion into them, the emptier they sounded.

The hardest part of all was invariably the last page—sometimes the last line. It was like watching your favorite Olympic figure skater who looks like she might actually win the gold medal if she can only land her last few jumps. The pressure mounts unbearably. This could be it, you think, this is the one. Then the crash on the final triple axel sends her bouncing and sprawling all over the ice.

Something similar happened with Sophia's Beethoven sonata, which just wouldn't come out right. After Take 3, when Sophia omitted two entire lines near the end, Istvan gently suggested that I go outside for some air. Istvan was very cool. He wore a black leather jacket, black ski cap, and black Clark Kent glasses. "There's a café down the street," he added. "Maybe you can get Sophia a hot chocolate. I could use some coffee myself." When I returned with the drinks fifteen minutes later, Istvan was packing up, and Sophia was laughing. They told me they'd gotten a Beethoven that was good enough—not error-free but very musical—and I was too relieved to question them.

We took the CD containing all of Sophia's attempts at each

piece and gave it to Wei-Yi, who made the final selections from all the takes ("the first Prokofiev, the third Liszt, and the final Beethoven, please"). Istvan then cut a submission CD, which we FedEx-ed to the competition.

And then we waited.

20

How You Get to

Carnegie Hall, Part 2

It was Lulu's turn! There is no rest for the Chinese mother, no time to recharge, no possibility of flying off with friends for a few days to mud springs in California. While we were waiting to hear back about Sophia's competition, I shifted my attention to Lulu, who was eleven at the time, and I had a great idea: As Mrs. Vamos had suggested, Lulu would audition for the Pre-College program at the Juilliard School in New York, open to highly talented kids between the ages of roughly seven and eighteen. Kiwon wasn't sure Lulu was quite ready technically, but I was confident we could get up to speed.

Jed disapproved and kept trying to change my mind. Juilliard Pre-College is famously intense. Every year, thousands of high-achieving kids from all over the world—especially Asia and most recently Russia and eastern Europe—try out for a handful of spots. The kids who apply do it because either (1) their dream is to become a professional musician; (2) their parents' dream is for them to become a professional musician; or (3) their parents think, correctly, that going to Juilliard will help them get into an Ivy League college. The lucky few who are accepted into the program study at Juilliard every Saturday for nine or ten hours.

Jed wasn't crazy about the idea of getting up at dawn every Saturday to drive to New York (I said I'd do it). But what he was really worried about was the pressure-cooker atmosphere and sometimes dog-eat-dog mentality that Juilliard is famous for. He wasn't sure that would be good for Lulu. Lulu wasn't sure it would be good for her either. In fact, she insisted that she didn't want to audition and wouldn't go even if she got in. But Lulu never wants to do anything I propose, so naturally I ignored her.

There was another reason Jed wasn't sure Juilliard was a good idea: Many years ago, he'd actually been a student there himself. After graduating from Princeton, he'd been accepted to Juilliard's Drama Division, notoriously even harder to get into than their world-famous Music Division. So Jed moved to New York City and studied acting with classmates who included Kelly McGillis (*Top Gun*), Val Kilmer (*Batman*), and Marcia Cross (*Desperate Housewives*). He dated ballet dancers, learned the Alexander Technique, and played the lead role in *King Lear*.

And then Jed got kicked out—for "insubordination." He was playing Lopakhin in Chekhov's *The Cherry Orchard,* and the director asked him to do something a certain way. Jed disagreed with her. Several weeks later, out of the blue at a rehearsal, she became furiously angry at Jed, snapping pencils in half, declaring that she couldn't work with someone who "just stands there, sneering at me, criticizing every word I say." Two days later, Jed was told by the chairman of the Drama Division (who happened to be married to the director Jed had offended) that he should find something else to do. After a year of waiting tables in New York, that something turned out to be Harvard Law School.

Maybe because I think it has a happy ending—Jed and I wouldn't have met if he'd stayed at Juilliard—I've told this story at party after party, where it's always a big hit, especially after I embellish it. People seem to think it's cool that a law professor went to Juilliard and knew Kevin Spacey (who was a few years ahead of Jed). There's also something about insubordination and getting kicked out that Americans love.

By contrast, when we told the story to my parents, it didn't go over well at all. This was before Jed and I were married. In fact, I had only recently revealed to them the fact of Jed's existence. After hiding him for two years, I had finally sprung on my parents that I was seriously dating Jed, and they were in shock. My mother was practically in mourning. When I was little, she'd given me lots of advice about how to find the right husband. "Don't marry anyone too handsome—dangerous. The most important things in a husband are moral character and health; if you marry a sickly man, you will have a terrible life." But she always assumed that the nonsickly husband would be Chinese, ideally someone Fukienese with an M.D./Ph.D.

Instead, here was Jed—white and Jewish. Neither of my parents found it remotely impressive that Jed had gone to drama school.

"Drama school?" repeated my father, unsmiling on the sofa where he and my mother were sitting side by side, staring at Jed. "You wanted to be an actor?"

The names Val Kilmer and Kelly McGillis didn't seem to mean anything to my parents, and they continued to sit stonily. But when Jed got to the part about being kicked out and having to work as a waiter for six months, my mother choked.

"*Kicked out?*" she said, throwing my father an anguished glance.

"Does that go on your record?" my father asked grimly.

"Dad, don't worry!" I laughed reassuringly. "It turned out to be a lucky thing. Jed ended up going to law school instead, and he loves the law. It's just a funny story."

"But now you say he's working for the government," my father said accusingly. I could tell he had a picture in his head of Jed in a booth stamping forms at the Department of Motor Vehicles.

For the third time, I patiently explained to my parents that Jed, wanting to do something in the public interest, had left his Wall Street law firm to work as a federal prosecutor at the U.S. Attorney's Office in the Southern District of New York. "It's really prestigious," I explained, "and it was *such* a hard job to get. Jed took an eighty percent pay cut for it."

"*Eighty percent!*" my mother burst out.

"Mom, it's only for three years," I said wearily, starting to give up. Among our Western friends, saying that Jed was taking a pay cut to do public service always brought "good-for-you's" and pats on the back. "If nothing else, it's important experience. Jed likes litigation. He might want to be a trial lawyer."

"Why?" my mother asked bitterly. "Because he wanted to be an *actor*?" This last word she spat out, as if it carried an indelible moral stain.

It's funny to think back on that now and how much my parents have changed since then. By the time I was thinking about Juilliard for Lulu, my parents idolized Jed. (Ironically, by then the son of one of our good family friends had become a famous actor in Hong Kong, and my parents' view about acting had totally changed too.) They had also figured out that Juilliard was famous ("Yo-Yo Ma!"). But like Jed, they didn't understand why I wanted Lulu to try for the Pre-College program.

"You don't want her to be a professional violinist, do you?" my father asked, puzzled.

I didn't have an answer, but that didn't stop me from being stubborn. Around the time that I submitted Sophia's CD to the piano competition, I submitted Lulu's application to Juilliard.

As I've said, raising kids the Chinese way is much harder than raising them the Western way. There is simply no respite. Just as I'd finally finished working with Sophia around the clock for two months on her pieces, I had to turn right around and do the same for Lulu.

The Juilliard Pre-College audition process is set up in a way that maximizes pressure. Applicants Lulu's age have to be prepared to play three octaves of major and minor scales and arpeggios, an étude, a slow and fast movement of a concerto, and another contrasting piece—all by memory, obviously. At the actual audition, the kids go into a room, without parents, and play before a panel of roughly five to ten Pre-College faculty members, who can ask to hear any part of any piece in any order and stop them at any time. The Pre-College violin faculty includes big names like Itzhak Perlman and the New York Philharmonic's concertmaster Glenn Dicterow, as well as some of the most prominent teachers of young violinists in the world. We had our eye on a teacher by the name of Naoko Tanaka, who, like Mrs. Vamos, was in the highest demand, with students from all over the world clawing to get into her studio. We knew of Miss Tanaka because Kiwon had studied with her for nine years, before going off at the age of seventeen to study with Mrs. Vamos.

It was especially hard to help Lulu prepare, because she was still maintaining that she would never in a million years do the audition. She hated everything she'd heard about it from Kiwon. She knew that some of the applicants would fly in from China, South Korea, and India just for the audition, which they'd been working toward for years. Others would have auditioned before and been rejected two or three times. Still others were already taking private lessons with Pre-College faculty members.

But I hunkered down. "It will be your decision in the end, Lulu," I lied. "We'll get prepared for the audition, but if in the end you really don't want to do it, you don't have to." "Never not try something out of fear," I would pontificate at other times. "Everything I've ever done that's valuable is something I was terrified to try." To improve productivity, I hired not only Kiwon for many hours a day but also a lovely Yale undergraduate named Lexie, whom Lulu came to adore. While Lexie didn't have Kiwon's technical ability, she played in the Yale orchestra and genuinely loved music. Intellectual and philosophical, Lexie was a wonderful influence on Lulu. She questioned things. She and Lulu would talk about their favorite composers and concertos, overrated violinists, and different interpretations of Lulu's pieces. After their conversations, Lulu would always be motivated to practice.

Meanwhile, I was still teaching my courses at Yale and finishing up a second book, this one about history's greatest empires and the secret to their success. I was also traveling continuously, giving lectures about democratization and ethnic conflict.

One day, when I was in an airport somewhere waiting to fly back to New Haven, I checked my BlackBerry and saw an e-mail from the sponsors of Sophia's piano competition. For a few minutes I was paralyzed, terrified of bad news. Finally, when I couldn't stand it any longer, I clicked the button.

Sophia was a first-prize winner. She was going to play at Carnegie Hall! There was just one problem: Sophia's Carnegie Hall performance was the evening before Lulu's Juilliard audition.

21

The Debut and the Audition

Sophia at Carnegie Hall, 2007

It was the big day—the day of Sophia's Carnegie Hall debut. This time I'd really gone wild. I'd spoken to Jed, and we decided to forgo our winter vacation for the year. Sophia's dress for the event was a charcoal satin floor-length gown from Barneys New York—no David's Bridal for this one! For the reception afterward, I'd rented out the Fontainebleau Room at the St. Regis New York, where we also took two rooms for two nights. In addition to sushi, crab cakes, dumplings, quesadillas, a raw oyster bar, and iced silver bowls of jumbo shrimp, I ordered a beef tenderloin station, a Peking duck station, and a pasta station (for the kids). At the last minute I had them throw in Gruyère profiteroles, Sicilian rice balls with wild mushrooms, and a giant dessert station. I'd also printed up invitations and sent them to everyone we knew.

Each time a new bill came, Jed's eyebrows shot up. "Well, there goes our summer vacation too," he said at one point. My mother, meanwhile, was horrified by my extravagance; growing up, we'd only ever stayed in a Motel 6 or Holiday Inn. But Carnegie Hall was a once-in-a-lifetime opportunity, and I was determined to make it unforgettable.

For analytical clarity, I should probably point out that some aspects of my behavior—for example, my tendency to show off and overdo things—are not characteristic of most Chinese mothers. I inherited those flaws, along with my loud voice and my love of big parties and the color red, from my father. Even when I was growing up, my mother, who's very muted and modest, would shake her head and say, "It's genetic. Amy's a clone of the oddball." The latter referred to my father, whom it's true I've always idolized.

Part of the deal I'd arranged with the St. Regis was that we'd have access to a piano, and the day before the recital Sophia and I practiced on and off throughout the day. Jed worried about me going too far and tiring out Sophia's fingers; Wei-Yi had told us that Sophia knew her pieces inside out and that being calm and focused was more important than anything. But I had to make sure that Sophia's performance was flawless, that she didn't leave out a single brilliant tiny nuance Wei-Yi had taught us. Contrary to everyone's advice, we practiced until almost 1:00 A.M. the night before. The last thing I said to her was, "You're going to be great. When you've worked as hard as you have, you know you've done everything you can, and it doesn't matter now what happens."

The next day when the moment came—while I could barely breathe, clutching the armrest of my seat in near rigor mortis—Sophia played brilliantly, jubilantly. I knew every note, every silence, every witty touch like the back of my hand. I knew where the potential pitfalls were; Sophia blew past them all. I knew her favorite parts, her most masterful transitions. I knew where thank goodness she didn't rush and exactly when she began to bring it home, allowing herself to improvise emotionally, knowing it was already a total triumph.

Afterward, when everyone else rushed to congratulate and hug her, I hung back. I didn't need the clichéd moment where "Sophia's eyes sought out mine in the crowd." I just watched my cute little grown-up girl from afar, laughing with her friends, piling up with flowers.

In moments of despair I force myself to relive that memory. My parents and sisters attended, as did Jed's father, Sy, and his wife, Harriet, and many friends and colleagues. Wei-Yi had come down from New Haven for the performance and was clearly proud of his young pupil. According to Sophia, it was one of the happiest days of her life. I had not only invited her entire grade, I rented a van to transport her schoolmates both ways between New Haven and New York. No one applauds as loudly as a bunch of giddy eighth-graders let loose in New York—and no one could possibly eat as much shrimp cocktail (which the St. Regis charged for by the piece).

As promised, here's the ending of Sophia's essay on "Conquering Juliet":

I didn't quite understand what was happening until I found myself backstage, petrified, quaking. My hands were cold. I couldn't remember how my piece started. An old mirror betrayed the contrast between my chalk-white face and my dark gown, and I wondered how many other musicians had stared into that same glass.

Carnegie Hall. It didn't seem right. This was supposed to be the unattainable goal, the carrot of false hope that would keep me practicing for an entire lifetime. And yet here I was, an eighth-grader, about to play "Juliet as a Young Girl" for the expectant crowd.

I had worked so hard for this. Romeo and Juliet weren't the only characters I had learned. The sweet, repetitive murmuring that accompanied Juliet was her nurse; the boisterous chords were Romeo's teasing friends. So much of me was manifested in this piece, in one way or another. At that moment, I realized how much I loved this music.

Performing isn't easy—in fact, it's heartbreaking. You spend months, maybe years, mastering a piece; you become a part of it, and it becomes a part of you. Playing for an audience is like giving blood; it leaves you feeling empty and a bit light-headed. And when it's all over, your piece just isn't yours anymore.

It was time. I walked out to the piano and bowed. Only the stage was lit, and I couldn't see the faces of the audience. I said good-bye to Romeo and Juliet, then released them into the darkness.

Sophia's success energized me, filled me with new dreams. I couldn't help noticing that the Weill Recital Hall, where Sophia played—while quite charming with its belle epoque arches and symmetrical proportions—was a relatively small venue, located on the third floor of Carnegie Hall. I learned that the much larger, magnificent hall that I'd seen on television, where some of the world's greatest musicians had played to audiences of nearly three thousand, was called the Isaac Stern Auditorium. I made a mental note that we ought to try to make it there someday.

There were a few shadows on the day. We all felt Florence's absence, which left a hollowness that couldn't be filled. It also stung a little that Sophia's old piano teacher Michelle didn't come; our move to Wei-Yi had not been taken well, despite our efforts to maintain a relationship. But the worst thing was that Lulu got food poisoning the day of the recital. After practicing her audition pieces all morning with Kiwon, they'd gone to a deli for lunch. Twenty minutes later, Lulu was sick to her stomach, convulsing with pain. She managed to make it through Sophia's performance before staggering out of the hall; Kiwon took her by taxi back to the hotel. Lulu missed the entire reception, and during the party Jed and I took turns running up to our hotel room, where Lulu vomited all night, with my mother attending to her.

The next morning, with Lulu white as a ghost and barely able to walk, we took her to Juilliard. She was wearing a yellow and white dress and a big bow in her hair, which only made her face look more drawn. I thought about canceling the audition, but we'd poured so many hours into preparing that even Lulu wanted to do it. In the waiting area, we saw Asian parents everywhere, pacing back and forth, grim-faced and single-minded. They seem so unsubtle, I thought to myself, can they possibly love music?

Then it hit me that almost all the other parents were foreigners or immigrants and that music was a ticket for them, and I thought, I'm not like them. I don't have what it takes.

When Lulu's name was called, and she walked bravely into the audition room by herself, my heart almost broke—I almost gave it all up right then. But instead, Jed and I plastered our ears to the door and listened as she played Mozart's Third Concerto and Gabriel Fauré's *Berceuse,* both as movingly as I'd ever heard her play. Afterward, Lulu told us that Itzhak Perlman and Naoko Tanaka, the famous violin teacher, had been among the judges in the room.

A month later we got the bad news in the mail. Jed and I knew the contents of the thin envelope instantly; Lulu was still at school. After reading the formal, two-line rejection letter, Jed turned away in disgust. He didn't say anything to me, but the unspoken accusation was, "Are you happy now, Amy? Now what?"

When Lulu came home, I said to her as cheerfully as I could, "Hey, Lulu, honey, guess what? We heard from Juilliard. They didn't accept you. But it doesn't matter—we didn't expect to get in this year. Lots of people don't get in their first time. Now we know what to do for next time."

I couldn't bear the look that flashed over Lulu's face. I thought for a second that she was going to cry, but then I realized she would never do that. How could I have set her up for such a disappointment? I thought to myself. All those hours we put in were now big black stains on our memory. And how would I ever get her to practice—

"I'm glad I didn't get in," Lulu's voice interrupted my thoughts. She looked a little angry now.

"Lulu, Daddy and I are so proud that—"

"Oh *stop it,*" Lulu snapped. "I told you—I don't care. You're the one who forced me to do it. I *hate* Juilliard. I'm happy I didn't get in," she repeated.

I'm not sure what I would have done if I hadn't received a call the next day from—of all people—Naoko Tanaka. Miss Tanaka said that she thought Lulu had auditioned wonderfully, showing unusual musicality, and that she herself had voted to accept Lulu. She also explained that a decision had been made that year to downsize the Pre-College violin program; as a result, an unprecedented number of applicants had competed for unprecedentedly few spots, making it even more difficult than usual to get in. I was just beginning to thank Miss Tanaka for her considerate call when she offered to take on Lulu as a student in her own private studio.

I was stunned. Miss Tanaka's private studio was famously exclusive—almost impossible to get into. My spirits soared, and I thought quickly. What I really wanted was a great teacher for Lulu; I didn't care that much about the Pre-College program. I knew that studying with Miss Tanaka would mean driving to New York City every weekend. I also wasn't sure how Lulu would react.

I accepted on Lulu's behalf on the spot.

22

Blowout in Budapest

Lulu and Sophia on stage at the Old Liszt Academy

After all those excruciating hours preparing for the Juilliard audition, and then the food poisoning and the rejection letter,
you'd think that I would have given Lulu a break. I probably
should have. But that was two years ago, when I was much
younger, and I didn't. Easing up would have been selling Lulu
short. It would have been the easy way out, which I saw as the
Western thing to do. Instead, I jacked up the pressure even

more. For the first time, I paid a real price, but nothing like the price I would eventually pay.

Two of the most important guests at Sophia's Carnegie Hall recital were Oszkár and Krisztina Pogány, old family friends from Hungary, who happened to be visiting New York at the time. Oszkár is a prominent physicist and my father's close friend. His wife, Krisztina, is a former concert pianist who is now very involved with the Budapest music scene. After Sophia's performance, Krisztina rushed up to us, raved about Sophia's playing—she'd especially liked her "Juliet as a Young Girl"—and said she had an inspiration.

Budapest, Krisztina explained, would soon be celebrating Museum Night, when museums all over the city would host lectures, performances, and concerts; for the price of a single ticket, people could "museum hop" late into the night. As part of Museum Night, the Franz Liszt Academy of Music would be presenting a number of concerts. Krisztina thought it would be a big hit to have a "Prodigy from America" concert, featuring Sophia.

It was a breathtaking invitation. Budapest is a famously musical city, the home of not only Liszt but Béla Bartók and Zoltán Kodály. Its stunning State Opera House is said to be surpassed acoustically only by Milan's La Scala and Paris's Palais Garnier. The venue Krisztina proposed for the concert was the Old Music Academy, an elegant three-story neo-Renaissance building that once served as the official residence of Franz Liszt, the founder and president of the academy. The Old Academy (replaced in 1907 by the New Academy of Music, located a few streets away) was now a museum filled with Liszt's original instruments, furniture, and handwritten musical scores. Krisztina told Sophia that she would perform on one of Liszt's own pianos! Also, the audience would be a large one—not to mention Sophia's first paying audience.

But I had a problem. So soon after the fanfare of Carnegie Hall, how would Lulu feel about another big event with Sophia as the center of attention? Lulu had been pleased with Miss Tanaka's offer; somewhat to my surprise, she immediately said she wanted to do it. But that did only a little to dull the sting of the Juilliard disappointment. To make matters worse, I hadn't thought to keep her audition a secret, and for months Lulu had to deal with people asking her, "Did you get the audition results yet? I'm *sure* you got in."

The Chinese parenting approach is weakest when it comes to failure; it just doesn't tolerate that possibility. The Chinese model turns on achieving success. That's how the virtuous circle of confidence, hard work, and more success is generated. I knew that I had to make sure Lulu achieved that success—at the same level as Sophia—before it was too late.

I came up with a plan and enlisted my mother as my agent. I asked her to call her old friend Krisztina and tell her all about Lulu and the violin: how she had played for Jessye Norman and then for the renowned violin instructor Mrs. Vamos, both of whom had said Lulu was terrifically talented, and finally, how Lulu had just been accepted as a private student by a world-famous teacher from the world-famous Juilliard School. I told my mother to feel out the possibility of having Lulu perform with Sophia as a duo in Budapest, even if only for one piece. Perhaps, I told my mother to suggest, that one piece could be Bartók's Romanian Folk Dances for Piano and Violin, which the girls had recently performed— and which I knew would appeal to Krisztina. Along with Liszt,

Bartók is Hungary's most famous composer, and his Folk Dances are sensational crowd-pleasers.

We lucked out. Krisztina, who had met Lulu and liked her fiery personality, told my mother that she loved the idea of having Sophia play a piece with her little sister and that the Romanian Dances would be a perfect addition to the program. Krisztina said she would arrange everything and even change the billing of the event to "Two Prodigy Sisters from America."

The girls' concert was set for June 23, only one month away. Once again, I bore down. There was a staggering amount of work to be done. I had exaggerated when I told my mother that the girls had recently performed the Romanian Dances; by "recently" I meant a year and a half ago. To relearn the Dances and get them just right, the girls and I had to work around the clock. Meanwhile, Sophia was also frantically practicing four other pieces Wei-Yi had chosen for her: Brahms's Rhapsody in G Minor, a piece by a Chinese woman composer, Prokofiev's *Romeo and Juliet,* and of course, one of Liszt's famous Hungarian Rhapsodies.

Although Sophia had the difficult repertoire, my real concern was Lulu. I wanted with all my heart for her to be dazzling. I knew that my parents would be at the concert; by coincidence, they were going to be in Budapest for the month of June because my father was being inducted into the Hungarian Academy of Sciences. I also didn't want to let Krisztina down. Most of all, I wanted Lulu to do well for Lulu. This is exactly what she needs, I thought to myself; it will give her so much confidence and pride if she does well. I had to deal with some resistance from Lulu: I had promised her time off after her audition no matter what, and now I was breaking that promise. But I steeled myself for battle, and when things got intolerable, I hired Kiwon and Lexie as auxiliaries.

Here's a question I often get: "But Amy, let me ask you this. Who are you doing all this pushing for—your daughters"—and here always the cocked head, the knowing tone—"or *yourself*?" I find this a very Western question to ask (because in Chinese thinking, the child is the extension of the self). But that doesn't mean it's not an important one.

My answer, I'm pretty sure, is that everything I do is unequiv-ocally 100% for my daughters. My main evidence is that so much of what I do with Sophia and Lulu is miserable, exhausting, and not remotely fun for me. It's not easy to make your kids work when they don't want to, to put in grueling hours when your own youth is slipping away, to convince your kids they can do something when they (and maybe even you) are fearful that they can't. "Do you know how many years you've taken off my life?" I'm constantly asking my girls. "You're both lucky that I have enormous longevity as indicated by my thick good-luck earlobes."

To be honest, I sometimes wonder if the question "Who are you really doing this for?" should be asked of Western parents too. Sometimes I wake up in the morning dreading what I have to do and thinking how easy it would be to say, "Sure Lulu, we can skip a day of violin practice." Unlike my Western friends, I can never say, "As much as it kills me, I just have to let my kids make their choices and follow their hearts. It's the hardest thing in the world, but I'm doing my best to hold back." Then they get to have a glass of wine and go to a yoga class, whereas I have to stay home and scream and have my kids hate me.

A few days before we left for Budapest, I e-mailed Krisztina, asking her if she knew of any experienced music teachers who could run through the Romanian Dances with the girls as a kind of dress rehearsal, perhaps offering some tips about how to play a Hungarian composer properly. Krisztina wrote back with good news. A prominent Eastern European violin teacher, whom I'll call Mrs. Kazinczy, had generously agreed to see the girls. Recently retired, Mrs. Kazinczy now taught only the most gifted violinists. She had a single slot available—on the day we arrived—and I grabbed it.

We arrived at our hotel in Budapest on the day before the concert, around ten in the morning—4:00 A.M. New Haven time. We were groggy and bleary-eyed. Jed and Lulu both had headaches. The girls just wanted to sleep, and I didn't feel so great myself, but unfortunately it was time for the lesson with Mrs. Kazinczy. We'd already received two messages, one from my parents and one from Krisztina, about where to meet. The four of us staggered into a taxi, and a few minutes later, we were at the New Academy of Music, a magnificent Art Nouveau building with majestic columns facing Franz Liszt Square and taking up almost half a block.

Mrs. Kazinczy met us in a large room on one of the upper floors. My parents and a beaming Krisztina were already there, sitting on chairs along one of the walls. There was an old piano in the room, which Krisztina signaled Sophia to go to.

Mrs. Kazinczy, to put it mildly, was high-strung. She looked like her husband had just left her for a younger woman but not before transferring all his assets to an offshore account. She subscribed to the strict Russian school of music teaching: impatient, demanding, and intolerant of anything she perceived as error. "No!" she yelled before Lulu had played a single note.

"What—why you hold bow like that?" she demanded incredulously. As the girls began playing, she stopped Lulu after every two notes, pacing back and forth, gesticulating wildly. She found the fingering Lulu had been taught monstrous and ordered her to correct it, even though it was the day before the performance. She also kept turning to the piano to snap at Sophia, although her main sights were set on Lulu.

I had a bad feeling. I could tell that Lulu found Mrs. Kazinczy's orders unreasonable, her reprimands unjust. The madder Lulu got, the more stiffly she played, and the less she was able to concentrate. Her phrasing deteriorated, followed by her intonation. Oh no, I thought, here it comes. Sure enough, at a certain point an irritated look came over Lulu, and suddenly she was no longer trying at all, no longer even listening. Meanwhile, Mrs. Kazinczy had worked herself into a frenzy. Her temples were bulging, and her voice got shriller. She kept saying things in Hungarian to Krisztina and getting alarmingly close to Lulu, talking in her face, poking her in the shoulder. At one moment of exasperation, Mrs. Kazinczy thwacked Lulu on her playing fingers with a pencil.

I saw the fury rising in Lulu. At home, she would have exploded immediately. But here, she struggled to hold it in, to keep playing. Mrs. Kazinczy wielded her pencil again. Two minutes later, in the middle of playing a passage, Lulu said she had to go to the bathroom. I got up quickly and went out with her into the hall, where after storming around a corner she burst into tears of rage.

"I won't go back in there," she said ferociously. "You can't make me. That woman is crazy—I hate her. I *hate* her!"

I didn't know what to do. Mrs. Kazinczy was Krisztina's

friend. My parents were still in the room. There were thirty more minutes left to the lesson, and everyone was waiting for Lulu to return.

I tried to reason with Lulu. I reminded her that Mrs. Kazinczy had said Lulu was incredibly talented, which is why she was demanding so much of her. ("I don't care!") I admitted that Mrs. Kazinczy was not good at communicating, but I said I thought she meant well and begged Lulu to give her another try. ("I won't!") When all else failed, I scolded Lulu. I said she had an obligation to Krisztina, who had gone out of her way to arrange the session, and to my parents, who would be horrified if she didn't go back. "You're not the only one involved, Lulu. You have to be strong and find a way to get through this. We all take a lot of things, Lulu—you can take this."

She refused. I was mortified. Unjustified as Mrs. Kazinczy may have been, she was still a teacher, an authority figure, and one of first things Chinese people learn is that you must respect authority. No matter what, you don't talk back to your parents, teachers, elders. In the end, I had to go back to the room alone, apologizing profusely and explaining (falsely) that Lulu was angry with *me*. I then made Sophia—who wasn't crazy about Mrs. Kazinczy either and who wasn't even a violinist—take the rest of the lesson, ostensibly getting tips about playing as a duo.

Back at the hotel, I yelled at Lulu, and afterward Jed and I got into an argument. He said that he didn't blame Lulu for leaving and that it was probably better that she had. He pointed out that she'd just been through the Juilliard audition, that she was exhausted with jet lag, and that she'd been whacked by a total stranger. "Isn't it a little strange for Mrs. Kazinczy to be trying to change Lulu's fingering the day before the concert? I thought you weren't supposed to do that," he said. "Maybe you should try being a little more sympathetic to Lulu. I know what you're trying to do, Amy. But if you don't watch out, everything might backfire."

Part of me knew that Jed was right. But I couldn't think about that. I had to stay focused on the concert. The next day, I was very severe with both girls, shuttling back and forth between their practice rooms at the New Academy.

Unfortunately, Lulu's outrage at Mrs. Kazinczy had only increased overnight. I could tell that she was replaying the episode in her head, getting more and more incensed and distracted. When I'd ask her to drill a passage, she'd suddenly burst out, "She didn't know what she was talking about—the fingering she suggested was ridiculous! Did you notice that she kept contradicting herself?" Or: "I don't think she understood Bartók at all; her interpretation was horrendous—who does she think she is?"

When I told her that she had to stop dwelling on Mrs. Kazinczy and wasting time, Lulu said, "You never take my side. And I don't want to perform tonight. I don't feel like it anymore. That woman wrecked everything. Just let Sophia perform alone." We fought all afternoon, and I was at wit's end.

In the end, I think Krisztina saved the day. When we arrived at the Old Music Academy, Krisztina rushed up to us, smiling and ebullient. She hugged the girls excitedly, gave them each a little gift, and said, "We are so very happy to have you. You are both so very ta*lent*ed"—she accented the second syllable. Shaking her head, Krisztina casually mentioned that Mrs. Kazinczy shouldn't have tried to change Lulu's fingering and that she must have forgotten the concert was the next day. "You are so ta*lent*ed,"

she repeated to Lulu. "It's going to be a wonderful performance!" Then she whisked them off—away from me—to a back
room, where she ran through parts of the program with them.

Up until the very last second I didn't know how things would
go—and whether I'd have one or two daughters performing that
night. But somehow, miraculously, Lulu pulled it out, and the
concert ended up being a spectacular success. The Hungarians,
a warm and generous people, gave the girls a standing ovation
and three bows, and the director of the museum invited them to
come back anytime. Afterward, we took the Pogánys, my parents, and Sy and Harriet, who had flown in just in time, out to a
celebration dinner.

But after that trip, something was different. For Lulu, the
experience with Mrs. Kazinczy was infuriating and outrageous,
violating her sense of right and wrong. It soured her on the Chinese model—if being Chinese meant having to take it from the
likes of Mrs. Kazinczy, then she didn't want any part of it. She'd
also tested what would happen if she simply refused to do what
her teacher and mother told her to do, and the sky hadn't fallen
in. On the contrary, she'd won. Even my parents, despite everything they'd drilled into me, sympathized with Lulu.

For my part, I felt that something had come loose, like the
unmooring of an anchor. I'd lost some control over Lulu. No
Chinese daughter would ever act the way Lulu did. No Chinese
mother would ever have allowed it to happen.

Part Three

Tigers are capable of great love, but they become too intense about it. They are also territorial and possessive. Solitude is often the price Tigers pay for their position of authority.

23

Pushkin

My two beautiful snow dogs

"Which one's ours?" Jed asked.

It was August 2008, and Jed and I were in Rhode Island. For reasons mysterious to everyone, including myself, I had insisted that we get a second dog, and we were at the same breeder's where we'd gotten Coco. Pacing around a rustic room with a wooden floor were three large, regal Samoyeds. Two of them, we learned, were the proud parents of the new litter; the third was the grandfather, worldly and magisterial at the venerable age of six. Scampering around the big dogs were four boisterous puppies, each an adorable yelping cottonball.

"Yours is the one over there," the breeder said, "under the stairs."

Turning around, Jed and I saw, standing in a different part of the room by itself, something that looked quite different from the other puppies. It was taller, leaner, less furry—and less cute. Its hind legs were two inches longer than its front legs, giving it an awkward tilt. Its eyes were narrow and very slanted; its ears, oddly protuberant. Its tail was longer and fuller than the others', but maybe because it was too heavy, it didn't curl up, but instead swung from side to side like a rat's tail.

"Are you sure that's a dog?" I asked dubiously. This wasn't as preposterous a question as it may sound. If anything, the creature most resembled a baby lamb, and given that the breeders raised some farm animals on their property, one easily could have wandered in.

But the breeder was sure. She winked at us, and said, "You'll see. She'll be a great beauty. She's got that great high Samoyed rear, just like her grandmother."

We brought our new puppy home and named her Pushkin— "Push" for short—even though she was a girl. When our family and friends first met her, they felt sorry for us. As a puppy, Push hopped like a bunny and stumbled over her own feet. "Can you return her?" my mother asked at one point, as she watched Push bump into walls and chairs. "I know what the problem is—she's blind," it dawned on Jed one day, and he raced her to the vet, who concluded that Push's eyesight was fine.

As Push grew bigger, she remained awkward, often tripping as she came down stairs. The trunk of her body was so long that she didn't seem to have full control over her back half, so she moved like a Slinky. At the same time, she was strangely limber; to this day, she likes to sleep with her stomach plastered against a cold floor and all four limbs splayed out. It's as if someone dropped her from the sky and she landed splat on the floor—in fact we call her "Splat" when we see her like that.

The breeder was right about one thing. Push was an ugly duckling. Within a year, she had transformed into a dog so breathtakingly magnificent that when we took walks cars constantly stopped short to marvel at her. She was bigger than Coco (who, due to the oddities of breeding, was actually Push's grandniece), with snow-white fur and exotic cat's eyes. Some dormant muscles had clearly developed because now her tail curled high up over her back like an enormous, lush plume.

But in terms of talent, Push stayed solidly in the lowest decile. Coco was not especially impressive, but compared to Push she was a genius. For some reason, Push—while even sweeter and gentler than Coco—couldn't do things that normal dogs could. She couldn't fetch and didn't like running. She kept getting stuck in funny places—under the sink, in berry bushes, halfway in and halfway out of the bathtub—and needing to be extricated. At first, I denied that there was anything different about Pushkin, and I spent hours trying to teach her to do things, but all to no avail. Oddly enough, Push seemed to love music. Her favorite thing to do was to sit next to Sophia's piano, singing (or in Jed's view, howling) along as Sophia played.

Despite her shortcomings, the four of us adored Push, just as we did Coco. In fact, her failings were what made her so endearing. "Oh-h-h, poor thing! What a cutie," we'd coo when she'd try to jump onto something and miss by a foot, and we'd rush to comfort her. Or we'd say, "Aw-w-w, just look at that. She can't see the Frisbee! She's so cu-u-ute." Initially, Coco was wary of her new sibling; we saw her testing Push in cagey ways. Push, by contrast, had a more limited range of emotions; wariness and caginess were not among them. She was content to follow Coco around amiably, avoiding any moves that required agility.

As sweet as Push was, it made absolutely no sense for our family to have a second dog, and no one knew it better than me. The distribution of dog responsibility in our household was 90% me, 10% the other three. Every day, starting at six in the morning, I was the one who fed, ran, and cleaned up after them; I also took them to all their grooming and vet appointments. To make matters worse, my second book had just been published, and in addition to teaching a full course load and working with the girls on their music, I was constantly flying around the country giving lectures. I'd always find ways to compress trips to D.C., Chicago, or Miami into one day. More than once, I got up at 3:00 A.M., flew to California and gave a lunch talk, then took the redeye home. "What were you thinking?" friends would ask me. "With so much on your plate already, why on earth would you get a second dog?"

My friend Anne thought there was a conventional explanation. "All my friends," she said, "get dogs the moment their kids become teenagers. They're preparing for the empty nest. Dogs are substitutes for children."

It's funny that Anne would say that, because Chinese parenting is nothing like dog raising. In fact it's kind of the opposite. For one thing, dog raising is social. When you meet other dog owners, you have lots to talk about. By contrast, Chinese parenting is incredibly lonely—at least if you're trying to do it in the

West, where you're on your own. You have to go up against an entire value system—rooted in the Enlightenment, individual autonomy, child development theory, and the Universal Declaration of Human Rights—and there's no one you can talk to honestly, not even people you like and deeply respect.

For example, when Sophia and Lulu were little, what I used to dread most was when other parents invited one of them over for a *playdate*. Why why why this terrible Western institution? I tried telling the truth once, explaining to another mother that Lulu had no free time because she had to practice violin. But the woman couldn't absorb this. I had to resort to the kinds of excuses that Westerners find valid: eye appointments, physical therapy, community service. At a certain point, the other mother got a hurt look on her face and began treating me icily, as if I thought Lulu were too good for her daughter. It really was a clash of worldviews. After fending off one playdate invitation, I couldn't believe it when another one would immediately come along. "How about Saturday?"—Saturday was the day before Lulu's lesson with Miss Tanaka in New York—"or two Fridays from today?" From their point of view, Western mothers just couldn't comprehend how Lulu could be busy every afternoon, for the whole year.

There's another huge difference between dog raising and Chinese parenting. Dog raising is easy. It requires patience, love, and possibly an initial investment of training time. By contrast, Chinese parenting is one of the most difficult things I can think of. You have to be hated sometimes by someone you love and who hopefully loves you, and there's just no letting up, no point at which it suddenly becomes easy. Just the opposite, Chinese parenting—at least if you're trying to do it in America, where all odds are against you—is a never-ending uphill battle, requiring a 24-7 time commitment, resilience, and guile. You have to be able to swallow pride and change tactics at any moment. And you have to be creative.

Last year, for instance, I had some students over for an end-of-the-semester party, one of my favorite things to do. "You're so nice to your students," Sophia and Lulu are always saying. "They have no idea what you're really like. They all think you're *nurturing* and *supportive*." The girls are actually right about that. I treat my law students (especially the ones with strict Asian parents) the exact opposite of the way I treat my kids.

On this occasion, the party was upstairs in our third-floor Ping-Pong room, which was also where Lulu practiced her violin. One of my students, named Ronan, found some practice notes I'd left for Lulu.

"What in the world—?" he said, reading the notes in disbelief. "Professor Chua, did you—did you *write this?*"

"Ronan, can you please put that down? And yes, I did write that," I admitted staunchly, not seeing any alternative. "I leave instructions like that every day for my violinist daughter, to help her practice when I'm not here."

But Ronan didn't seem to be listening. "Oh, my god—there's more," he said, incredulous. And he was right. Lying around were dozens of instruction sheets, some typed, some handwritten, that I'd forgotten to hide. "I can't believe it. These are so— *weird.*"

I didn't think they were weird. But you can judge for yourself. Here are three unedited examples of the daily practice notes I wrote up for Lulu. Just ignore the nutty titles; I made those up to attract Lulu's attention. By the way, in the second one, the "m." means "measure"—so yes, I'm giving measure-by-measure instructions.

CHOW CHOW LeBOEUF
Installation One.

Only 55 minutes!!
HELLO LULU!!! You are doing great. Light!! Light!!!! LIGHT!!!
APOLLO Mission: Keeping violin in the position that allows it to stay up by itself sans hands, even on hard parts.

15 minutes: SCALES. High, light fingers. LIGHT, ringing bow.
15 minutes: Schradieck: (1) Higher lighter fingers. (2) Hand position, so pinky always stands up and hovers. Do the whole thing with metronome once. Then DRILL hard sections, 25x each. Then do whole thing again.

15 minutes: Kreutzer octaves. Pick ONE new one. Do it slowly first – INTONATION – 2x.

CHALLENGE OF THE DAY:

10 minutes: Kreutzer #32. Work it through YOURSELF, with a metronome. SLOW. Light bows. If you can do this, you rock.

LOS BOBOS DI MCNAMARA – BRUCH CONCERTO

GOALS: (1) KEEP YOUR VIOLIN UP! Especially during chords! (2) *articulation* – focus on making the "little" notes clear and bright – use quicker, lighter fingers (standing up more) (3) shaping passages; dynamics – start with slower bow and get faster

<u>DRILLS</u>

PAGE 7
Opening measures: mm. 18 & 19:
    (a) Use ½ the bow pressure & faster bow on chords. Lower elbow. ***Keep violin still***!
    (b) Drill little notes (da da dum) to make them clear – drop fingers more quickly and relax them more quickly
m. 21:   (a) triplets on the string – 25x each!
    (b) make 8th notes clearer – drill! RELAX fingers after tapping!
mm. 23-6: Again, ½ bow pressure on chords and clearer, faster fingers on short notes
mm 27-30: IMPORTANT: This line is too heavy, and your violin drops! Super light chord. Clearer articulation. MORE the second time.
m. 32: Drop fingers from higher and relax them quicker. Keep violin and head still on the run.
m. 33: Faster bow, lighter! Circle off (up!)!

PAGE 8
m. 40: This chord is way too heavy! ½ bow pressure and high violin! Articulate short notes.
m. 44: This chord should still be light, even though more sound – use a faster bow!
mm 44-5 – soft hand, soft wrist
mm 48-49 – make this more lively! Faster, lighter fingers! Stand them up but relax them!
m. 52 – articulation!
mm. 54-58 – each one should get LONGER BOWS! More exciting – grow!
m. 78 – higher fingers! Don't push – keep fingers light!
m. 82 – really crescendo, start slow then faster bow! Then drop quieter and crescendo huge! FIRST run is ***TAYLOR SWIFT***! SECOND run is ***LADY GAGA!!*** THIRD run is ***BEYONCE!!***
m. 87 – more direction, follow the phrase (louder going up, quieter going down)

PAGE 9:
mm. 115-6 – start with less bow and lots of bow on the high A. Direction!
m. 131 get quiet!
mm.136 -145 – really SHAPE this (louder and more bow when you go UP, quieter coming down) Drill out-of-tune notes, 50x each
mm. 146-159 tranquillo but GOOD articulation
mm. 156-158 – keep crescendoing
m. 160-161 – articulation

PAGE 10
m. 180: Practice entrance. Direction! Start w/ slower bow, then get faster, most on high B!
m. 181-83: drill clear articulation – quick, light fingers!
m. 185: ½ the bow speed on chords – lighter! Clearer little notes (da-da-dum) – quicker finger
m. 193-195 – DRILL shifts – exact position! 50x
m. 194: Start less, then really crescendo!
m. 200 – memorize correct notes – drill 30x
m. 202 – practice chords – exact hand position – intonation!
m. 204 use very soft hand and relaxed wrist!

SPUNKY PICKS – ALOHA STREAM 7
MENDELSSOHN!

Perpetual Mobile
Page 2
Opening:
  *On crescendo, energy goes up!
  *Also, it goes up 3 times, make them different – maybe LESS on last one
  * Last measure of line 2 is DIFFERENT HARMONY – so bring that out
Line 3: Bring out melody notes, less on repeated notes. Then "rolling down"
Line 4: Make sure to play important notes with MUCH LONGER BOW
Line 5: Bring out WEIRD notes
Line 6: So many As! Boring – so make them quieter and bring out the OTHER notes.
Line 7: Huge long 2-octave scale – start LESS and make a huge crescendo!!

Page 3
Line 5: At the f, use almost the entire bow – make it exciting! – then diminuendo to tiny
Line 6-7: Follow pattern – less, then suddenly EXPLOSION at f!
Line 8-9: same thing – quiet and then sudden EXPLOSION at f!
Line 10: Bring out TOP 2 notes, bottom note less important.

Mendelssohn
Opening:
  Andante –a bit faster
  Make this much more relaxed, intimate, like you are ALL ALONE WITH SLEEPING DOGS.
  Same thing happens 2x, then BRING OUT the 3rd time –open up a bit!
Line 4: Now, a little more worried, tense. MAYBE ONE SLEEPING DOG SEEMS SICK?
Line 5: MUCH MORE ENERGY ON HIGHEST note! The gradually bring it back to gentle, same low energy, relaxed like beginning.

MIDDLE SECTION:

  100% different character – SCARY!
  Use very FAST BOW! Much more energy! WHOLE bow in some parts.
  Change bow speed!!
  Last 3 lines, going up little by little So start with less bow –and INCREASE by 1.5 inch each time.
  Line -2. P, then forte! Bring out nervous character!

Page 11, line 1: More intense! Crescendo to high point!!

I have hundreds, maybe thousands of these. They have a long history. Even when the girls were little, because I tended to be too harsh in person, I'd leave little notes for them everywhere—on their pillows, in their lunch boxes, on their music scores—saying things like, "Mommy has a bad temper, but Mommy loves you!" or, "You are Mommy's pride and joy!"

With dogs, you don't have to do anything like this. And if you did, they probably couldn't understand it anyway, especially not Pushkin.

My dogs can't do anything—and what a relief. I don't make any demands of them, and I don't try to shape them or their future. For the most part, I trust them to make the right choices for themselves. I always look forward to seeing them, and I love just watching them sleep. What a great relationship.

24

Rebellion

Lulu, age thirteen

The Chinese virtuous circle didn't work with Lulu. I just couldn't understand it. Everything seemed to be going exactly according to plan. At considerable cost—but nothing I wasn't prepared to pay—Lulu succeeded in all the ways I'd always dreamed she would. After months of grueling preparation and the usual fights, threats, and yelling and screaming at home, Lulu auditioned for and won the position of concertmaster of a prestigious youth orchestra, even though she was only twelve and much younger than most of the other musicians. She received a statewide "prodigy" award and made the newspapers. She got straight As and won her school's top French and Latin recitation prizes. But instead of her success producing confidence, gratitude toward parents, and the desire to work harder, the opposite happened. Lulu started rebelling: not just against practicing, but against everything I'd ever stood for.

Looking back, I think things started to turn when Lulu was in sixth grade—I just didn't realize it. One of the things Lulu hated most was my insistence on pulling her out of school to get in some extra violin practicing. I felt they wasted a lot of time at Lulu's school, so several times a week I'd write a note to her teacher explaining that she had a recital or an audition coming up and requesting permission to take her out of school during lunch period or gym class. Sometimes I'd be able to cobble together a two-hour block by combining lunch, two recesses, and, say, music class, where they'd be playing cowbells, or art class, where they'd be decorating booths for the Halloween Fair. I could see that Lulu dreaded the sight of me every time I appeared at her school, and her classmates always looked at me oddly, but she was only eleven then, and I could still impose my will on her. And I'm sure it was because of the extra practicing that Lulu won all those music honors.

It wasn't easy on my end either. I'd be having office hours with my students, then suddenly have to excuse myself for a "meeting." I'd race to Lulu's school to pick her up, race to Kiwon's apartment to drop her off, then race back to my office, where there would be a line of students waiting for me. Half an hour later, I'd have to excuse myself again to return Lulu to school, then I'd screech back to my own office for another three hours of meetings. The reason I took Lulu to Kiwon's rather than supervise her practicing myself was that I didn't think she'd resist Kiwon, and certainly not fight with her. After all, Kiwon wasn't family.

One afternoon, just fifteen minutes after I'd dropped Lulu off, I got a call from Kiwon. She sounded flustered and frustrated. "Lulu doesn't want to play," she said. "Maybe you'd better come pick her up." When I got there, I apologized profusely to Kiwon, mumbling something about Lulu being tired because she hadn't gotten enough sleep. But it turned out that Lulu hadn't just refused to play. She'd been rude to Kiwon, talking back, challenging her advice. I was mortified and disciplined Lulu severely at home.

But things got worse as time went on. Whenever I arrived at Lulu's school to pick her up, her face would darken. She'd turn her back on me and say she didn't want to leave. When I finally got her to Kiwon's place, she'd sometimes refuse to get out of the car. If somehow I succeeded in getting her up to Kiwon's apartment—by then there might be only twenty minutes left—she'd either refuse to play or purposely play badly, out of tune or with no emotion. She'd also deliberately provoke Kiwon, slowly infuriating her, then maddeningly asking, "What's wrong? Are you okay?"

Once, in passing, Kiwon let slip that her boyfriend, Aaron, after witnessing a practice session, had said, "If I had a daughter I'd never allow her to act like that—to be so disrespectful."

That was a slap. Aaron, who'd always adored Lulu, was as easygoing as they come. He was raised in the most liberal and lenient of Western households, where the kids didn't get in trouble for skipping school and did pretty much anything they wanted. And yet he was criticizing my parenting, my daughter's behavior—and he was totally right.

Around the same time, Lulu started talking back to me and openly disobeying me in front of my parents when they visited. This might not sound like a big deal to Westerners, but in our household it was like desecrating a temple. In fact, it was so out of the realm of the acceptable that no one knew what to do. My father pulled me aside and privately urged me to let Lulu give up the violin. My mother, who was close to Lulu (they were e-mail pen pals), told me flat out, "You have to stop being so stubborn, Amy. You're too strict with Lulu—too extreme. You're going to regret it."

"Why are you turning on me now?" I shot back. "This is how you raised me."

"You can't do what Daddy and I did," my mother replied. "Things are different now. Lulu's not you—and she's not Sophia. She has a different personality, and you can't force her."

"I'm sticking to the Chinese way," I said. "It works better. I don't care if nobody supports me. You've been brainwashed by your Western friends."

My mother just shook her head. "I'm telling you, I'm worried about Lulu," she said. "There's something wrong in her eyes." This hurt me more than anything.

Instead of a virtuous circle, we were in a vicious spiral downward. Lulu turned thirteen and grew more alienated and resentful. She wore a constant apathetic look on her face, and every other word out of her mouth was "No" or "I don't care." She rejected my vision of a valuable life. "Why can't I hang out with my friends like everyone else does?" she'd demand. "Why are you so against shopping malls? Why can't I have sleepovers? Why does every second of my day have to be filled up with work?"

"You're concertmaster, Lulu," I'd reply. "It's a great honor they've given you, and you have a huge responsibility. The entire orchestra is counting on you."

Lulu would respond, "Why am I in this family?"

The odd thing was that Lulu actually loved orchestra. She had lots of friends, she liked being a leader, and she had great chemistry with the conductor, Mr. Brooks. I'd see her joking around and laughing spiritedly at rehearsals—maybe because rehearsal was time away from me.

Meanwhile, the disagreements between Jed and me were growing. Privately, he'd tell me furiously to show more restraint or to stop making crazy overgeneralizations about "Westerners" and "Chinese people." "I know you think you do people a huge favor by criticizing them, so that they can improve themselves," he'd say, "but have you ever considered that you just make people feel bad?" His biggest criticism was "Why do you insist on saying such glowing things about Sophia in front of Lulu all the time? How do you think that makes Lulu feel? Can't you see what's happening?"

"I refuse to cheat Sophia out of praise she deserves, just to 'protect Lulu's feelings,'" I'd say, infusing the last three words with as much sarcasm as I could muster. "This way, Lulu knows I think she's every bit as good as Sophia. She doesn't need affirmative action."

But apart from intervening occasionally to defuse blowups, Jed always took my side in front of the girls. From the beginning, we'd had a united-front strategy, and despite his misgivings, Jed didn't go back on it. Instead, he tried his best to bring balance to the family, making us go on family biking trips, teaching the girls how to play poker and pool, reading them science fiction, Shakespeare, and Dickens.

Then Lulu did something else unimaginable: She went public with her insurgency. As Lulu well knew, Chinese parenting in the West is an inherently closet practice. If it comes out that you push your kids against their will, or want them to do better than other kids, or god forbid ban sleepovers, other parents will heap opprobrium on you, and your children will pay the price. As a result, immigrant parents learn to conceal things. They learn to look jovial in public and pat their kids on the back and say things like, "Good try, buddy!" and "Go team spirit!" No one wants to be a pariah.

That's why Lulu's maneuver was so smart. She'd argue loudly with me on the street, at a restaurant, or in stores, and strangers would turn their heads to stare when they heard her say things like, "Leave me alone! I don't like you. Go away." When friends were over for dinner and asked her how her violin playing was going, she'd say, "Oh, I have to practice all the time. My mom makes me. I don't have a choice." Once she screamed so loudly in a parking lot—she was enraged at something I'd said and refused to get out of the car—that she attracted the attention of a policeman, who came over to see "what the problem was."

Oddly enough, school remained an inviolable bastion—Lulu left me that much. When Western kids rebel, their grades typically suffer, and occasionally they even flunk out. By contrast, as a half-Chinese rebel, Lulu continued to be a straight-A student, liked by all her teachers and repeatedly described in report cards as generous, kind, and helpful to other students. "Lulu is a joy," one of her teachers wrote. "She is perceptive and compassionate, a favorite among her classmates."

But Lulu saw it differently. "I have no friends. No one likes me," she announced one day.

"Lulu, why do you say that?" I asked anxiously. "Everyone likes you. You're so funny and pretty."

"I'm ugly," Lulu retorted. "And you don't know anything. How can I have any friends? You won't let me do anything. I can't go anywhere. It's all your fault. You're a freak."

Lulu refused to help run the dogs. She refused to take out the garbage. It was glaringly unfair for Sophia to do chores and not Lulu. But how do you physically make someone five feet tall do something they don't want to do? This problem is not supposed to come up in Chinese households, and I had no answer. So I did the only thing I knew: I fought fire with fire. I gave not one inch. I called her a disgrace as a daughter, to which Lulu replied, "I know, I know. You've told me." I told her she ate too much. ("Stop it. You're diseased.") I compared her to Amy Jiang, Amy Wang, Amy Liu, and Harvard Wong—all first-generation Asian kids—none of whom ever talked back to their parents. I asked her what I had done wrong. Had I not been strict enough? Given her too much? Allowed her to mix with bad-influence kids? ("Don't you dare insult my friends.") I told her I was thinking of adopting a third child from China, one who would practice when I told her to, and maybe even play the cello in addition to the violin and piano.

"When you're eighteen," I would shout as she stalked away from me up the stairs, "I'll let you make all the mistakes you want. But until then, I will not give up on you."

"I *want* you to give up on me!" Lulu yelled back more than once.

When it came to stamina, Lulu and I were evenly matched. But I had an advantage. I was the parent. I had the car keys, the bank account, the right not to sign permission slips. And that was all under U.S. law.

"I need a haircut," Lulu said one day.

I replied, "After you spoke to me so rudely and refused to play the Mendelssohn musically, you expect me to get in the car now and drive you where you want?"

"Why do I have to bargain for everything?" Lulu asked bitterly.

That night, we had another big argument, and Lulu locked herself in her room. She refused to come out and wouldn't answer when I tried to talk to her through the door. Much later, from my study, I heard the click of her door unlocking. I went to see her and found her sitting calmly on her bed.

"I think I'm going to go to sleep now," she said in a normal voice. "I've finished all my homework."

But I wasn't listening. I was staring at her.

Lulu had taken a pair of scissors and cut her own hair. On one side, it hung unevenly to about her chin. On the other, it was chopped off above the ear in an ugly, jagged line.

My heart skipped a beat. I almost exploded at her, but something—I think it was fear—made me hold my tongue.

A moment passed.

"Lulu—" I began.

"I like short hair," she interrupted.

I glanced away. I couldn't stand to look at her. Lulu had always had hair that everyone envied: wavy, brown-black—a Chinese-Jewish special. Part of me wanted to scream hysterically at Lulu and throw something at her. Another part of me wanted to wrap my arms around her and cry uncontrollably.

Instead, I said calmly, "I'll make an appointment with a hair salon first thing in the morning. We'll find someone to fix it."

"Okay." Lulu shrugged.

Later, Jed said to me, "Something has to change, Amy. We have a serious problem."

For the second time that night, I felt like crying uncontrollably. But instead, I rolled my eyes. "It's not a big deal, Jed," I said. "Don't create a problem where there isn't one. I can handle this."

25

Darkness

My little sister Katrin and me in the early eighties

When I was growing up, one of my favorite things was to play with my third sister, Katrin. Maybe because she was seven years younger than me, there was no rivalry or conflict. She was also preposterously cute. With her shiny black eyes, her shiny bowl haircut, and her rosebud lips, she was constantly attracting the attention of strangers, and once won a JCPenney photo contest that she hadn't even entered. Because my mother was often busy with my youngest sister, Cindy, my second sister, Michelle, and I took turns taking care of Katrin.

I have great memories from those days. I was bossy and confident, and Katrin idolized her big sister, so it was a perfect fit. I made up games and stories, and taught her how to play jacks and Chinese hopscotch and how to jump rope double Dutch. We played restaurant; I was the chef and the waiter, and she was the customer. We played school; I was the teacher, and she, along with five stuffed animals, was my student (Katrin excelled at my courses). I held McDonald's carnivals to raise money for muscular dystrophy; she manned the booths and collected money.

Thirty-five years later, Katrin and I were still close. The two of us were the most alike of the four sisters, at least on the surface. She and I both had two Harvard degrees (actually, she had three, because of her M.D./Ph.D.), we both married Jewish men, we both went into academics like our father, and we both had two children.

A few months before Lulu chopped off her hair, I got a call from Katrin, who taught and ran a lab out at Stanford. It was the worst call I have ever received in my life.

She was sobbing. She told me that she had been diagnosed with a rare, almost certainly fatal leukemia.

Impossible, I thought confusedly. Leukemia striking my family—my lucky family—for a second time?

But it was true. Katrin had been feeling exhausted, nauseated, and short of breath for several months. When she finally saw a doctor, the results of the blood tests were unmistakable. In a cruel coincidence, the leukemia she had was caused by the very kind of cell mutation she was studying in her lab.

"I'm probably not going to live very long," she said, crying. "What's going to happen to Jake? And Ella won't even know me." Katrin's son was ten, her daughter barely one. "You have to make sure she knows who I was. You have to promise me, Amy. I better get some pictures——" And she broke off.

I was in shock. I just couldn't believe it. An image of Katrin at ten flashed into my head, and it was impossible to put that together with the word *leukemia*. How could this be happening to Katrin——*Katrin*? And my parents! How could they take this——it would kill them.

"Exactly what did the doctors say, Katrin?" I heard myself asking in a strangely confident voice. I had snapped into my big-sister, can-do, invulnerable mode.

But Katrin didn't answer. She said she had to get off the phone and would call me again.

Ten minutes later, I got an e-mail from her. It said: "Amy, it's really really bad. Sorry! I'll need chemotherapy then bone marrow transplant if possible, then more chemo, and low chance of survival."

Being a scientist, she of course was right.

26

Rebellion, Part 2

I took Lulu to a salon the day after she cut her hair. We didn't speak much in the car. I was tense and had a lot on my mind.

"What happened?" the hairdresser asked.

"She cut it," I explained. I had nothing to hide. "Is there anything you can do to make it look better while it grows out?"

"Wow—you did a real job on yourself, honey," the woman said to Lulu, eyeing her curiously. "What made you do this?"

"Oh, it was an act of adolescent self-destruction aimed primarily at my mother," I thought Lulu might say. She certainly had the vocabulary and the psychological self-awareness to do so.

But instead, Lulu said in a pleasant voice, "I was trying to layer it. But I really messed up."

Later, back home, I said, "Lulu, you know that Mommy loves you, and everything I do, I do for you, for your future."

My own voice sounded artificial to me, and Lulu must have

thought so too, because her response was, "That's great," in a flat, apathetic tone.

Jed's fiftieth birthday came up. I organized a huge surprise party, inviting old friends from his childhood and every part of his life. I asked everyone to bring a funny story about Jed. Weeks in advance, I asked Sophia and Lulu each to write her own toast.

"It can't just be tossed off," I ordered. "It has to be meaningful. And it can't be clichéd."

Sophia got right on it. As usual, she didn't consult me or ask my advice on a single word. By contrast, Lulu said, "I don't want to give a toast."

"You *have* to give a toast," I replied.

"No one my age gives toasts," Lulu said.

"That's because they're from bad families," I retorted.

"Do you know how crazy you sound?" Lulu asked. "They're not from 'bad' families. What's a 'bad' family?"

"Lulu, you are so ungrateful. When I was your age, I worked nonstop. I built a treehouse for my sisters because my father asked me to. I obeyed everything he said, and that's why I know how to use a chainsaw. I also built a hummingbird house. I was a newspaper carrier for the *El Cerrito Journal* and had to wear a huge fifty-pound pouch over my head stuffed with papers and walk five miles. And look at you—you've been given every opportunity, every privilege. You've never had to wear imitation Adidas with four stripes instead of three. And you can't even do this one tiny thing for Daddy. It's disgusting."

"I don't want to give a toast," was Lulu's response.

I pulled out the big guns. I threatened everything I could think of. I bribed her. I tried to inspire her. I tried to shame her. I offered to help her write it. I jacked up the stakes and gave her an ultimatum, knowing it was a pivotal battle.

When the party came, Sophia delivered a minimasterpiece. At sixteen, standing 5' 8" in her heels, she had become a stunning girl with a sly wit. In her toast, she captured her father perfectly, gently poking fun but ultimately lionizing him. Afterward, my friend Alexis came up to me. "Sophia is just unbelievable."

I nodded. "She gave a great toast."

"Absolutely . . . but that's not what I meant," said Alexis. "I don't know if people really get Sophia. She's totally her own person. Yet she always manages to do your family proud. And that Lulu is just adorable."

I hadn't found Lulu adorable at all. During Sophia's toast, Lulu stood next to her sister, smiling affably. But she had written nothing, and she refused to say a single word.

I had lost. It was the first time. Through all the turbulence and warfare in our household, I'd never lost before, at least not on something important.

This act of defiance and disrespect infuriated me. My anger simmered for a while, then I unleashed my full wrath. "You've dishonored this family—and yourself," I said to Lulu. "You're going to have to live with your mistake for the rest of your life."

Lulu snapped back, "You're a show-off. It's all about you. You already have one daughter who does everything you want. Why do you need me?"

There was now a wall between us. In the old days, we'd fight ferociously but always make up. We'd end up snuggling in her bed or mine, hugging each other, giggling as we imitated ourselves arguing. I'd say things totally inappropriate for a parent, like "I'm going to be dead soon" or "I can't believe you love me so much it hurts." And Lulu would say, "Mommy! You are so weird!" but smile despite herself. Now Lulu stopped coming to my room at night. She directed her anger at not just me but also Jed and Sophia, and spent more and more time holed up in her room.

Don't think I didn't try to win Lulu back. When I wasn't furious or fighting with her, I'd do everything I could. Once I said, "Hey Lulu! Let's change our lives and do something totally different and fun—let's have a garage sale." And we did (net earnings $241.35), and it was fun, but it didn't change our lives. Another time, I suggested she try a lesson on the electric violin. She did, and liked it, but when I tried to book a second lesson, she told me it was stupid and to stop. Before long we'd be at it again, locked in hostility.

On the other hand, for two people who were constantly at each other's throats, Lulu and I spent a lot of time together, although I wouldn't exactly call it quality time. This was our usual weekend drill:

Saturday: 1 hour drive (at 8:00 A.M.) to Norwalk, CT
     3 hour orchestra practice
     1 hour drive back to New Haven
     Homework
     1–2 hours violin practice
     1 hour fun family activity (optional)

Sunday: 1–2 hours violin practice
    2 hour drive to New York City
    1 hour lesson with Miss Tanaka

2 hour drive back to New Haven

Homework

In retrospect, it was pretty miserable. But there was a flip side that made it all worthwhile. The thing is, Lulu hated the violin— except when she loved it. Lulu once said to me, "When I play Bach, I feel like I'm time traveling; I could be in the eighteenth century." She told me that she loved how music transcended history. At one of Miss Tanaka's biannual recitals, I remember Lulu mesmerizing the audience with Mendelssohn's Violin Concerto. Afterward, Miss Tanaka said to me, "Lulu's different from the others. She really feels the music and understands it. You can tell she loves the violin."

Part of me felt as if we had pulled the wool over Miss Tanaka's eyes. But another part of me was filled with inspiration and new resolve.

Lulu's Bat Mitzvah approached. Even though I'm not Jewish and the Bat Mitzvah was Jed's terrain, Lulu and I went to battle here too. I wanted her to play the violin at her Bat Mitzvah. I had in mind Joseph Achron's "Hebrew Melody," a beautiful, prayerful piece that Lulu's old friend Lexie had told us about. Jed approved; Lulu didn't.

"*Play violin?* At my Bat Mitzvah? That's ridiculous! I refuse," Lulu said, incredulous. "It's completely inappropriate. Do you even know what Bat Mitzvah means? It's not a recital." Then she added, "I just want to have a big party, and get lots of presents."

This was said to provoke and enrage me. Lulu had heard me railing for years against spoiled rich kids whose parents spend millions of dollars on their Bat Mitzvah parties, cotillions, or sweet sixteens. The truth is that Lulu has a strong Jewish identity. Unlike Sophia (or for that matter, Jed), Lulu had always insisted on observing Passover rules and fasting on Yom Kippur. For her, even more than for Sophia, the Bat Mitzvah was an important event in her life, and she threw herself with a passion into learning her Hebrew Torah and haftarah portions.

I wouldn't take the bait. "If you don't play the violin," I said calmly, "then Daddy and I won't throw you a party. We can just have a small ceremony—it's the ritual that's important, after all."

"You have no right!" Lulu said furiously. "That's so unfair. You didn't make Sophia play the piano at her Bat Mitzvah."

"It's good for you to do something that Sophia didn't," I said.

"You're not even Jewish," Lulu retorted. "You don't know what you're talking about. This has nothing to do with you."

Six weeks before the date, I sent out Lulu's invitations. But I warned her, "If you don't play the 'Hebrew Melody,' I'll cancel the party."

"You can't do that," Lulu said scornfully.

"Why don't you try me, Lulu?" I dared her. "See if I'll do it or not."

I honestly didn't know who'd win this one. It was a high-risk maneuver too, because I didn't have an exit strategy if I lost.

27

Katrin

The news about Katrin's cancer was unbearable for my parents. Two of the strongest people I know, they simply crumpled in grief. My mother cried all the time and wouldn't leave her house or respond to calls from friends. She wouldn't even talk to Sophia and Lulu on the phone. My father kept calling me, his voice anguished, asking me—over and over—if there was any hope.

For treatment, Katrin chose the Dana-Farber/Harvard Cancer Center in Boston. We'd learned that it was one of the best bone marrow transplant facilities in the country. Harvard was also where Katrin and her husband, Or, had studied and trained, and she still knew people there.

Everything happened so fast. Just three days after getting her diagnosis, Katrin and Or locked up their house at Stanford and moved their entire household to Boston (Katrin refused even to consider leaving her children behind in California with their grandparents). With the help of our friends Jordan and Alexis, we found them a house to rent in Boston, a school for Jake, and day care for Ella.

Katrin's leukemia was so aggressive that the doctors at Dana-Farber told her she had to go straight to a bone marrow transplant. No other route offered any chance of survival. But for the transplant to be possible, Katrin had to overcome two huge hurdles. First, she had to undergo intensive chemotherapy and pray that her leukemia would go into remission. Second, if it did, she had to get lucky and find a donor match. For each of these hurdles, the chances of success weren't great. For both to succeed, the odds were terrifying. And even if all that worked out, the chances of surviving the bone marrow transplant were even worse.

Katrin had two days in Boston before she checked into the hospital. I was there when she said good-bye to her children. She'd insisted on doing the laundry—two loads—and she'd laid out Jake's clothes for the next day. I watched in paralyzed incredulity as she carefully folded her son's shirts and smoothed her daughter's bibs and onesies. "I love doing laundry," she said to me. Before she left the house, she gave me all her jewelry for safekeeping. "In case I don't make it back," she said.

Or and I drove Katrin to the hospital. While we were waiting to fill out forms, she kept joking around—"Get me a good wig, Amy. I've always wanted nice hair"—and apologizing for taking up so much of my time. When we finally got to her hospital room— on the other side of a curtain was a deathly-looking elderly woman who'd obviously been through some chemotherapy—the first thing Katrin did was put up pictures of her family. There was a close-up of Ella, one of Jake at age three, and one of the four of them beaming on a tennis court. Although she looked distracted now and then, Katrin seemed completely calm and deliberate.

By contrast, when two medical interns—one was Asian, the other Nigerian—came to introduce themselves to Katrin, I was overwhelmed with indignation and rage. It was as if they were playing doctor. They had no answers to any of our questions, they twice referred to the wrong kind of leukemia, and Katrin ended up having to explain to them the protocol they needed to follow that night. All I could think was, Students? My sister's life is in the hands of medical students?

But Katrin's reaction was totally different. "I can't believe that the last time I was in this building, I was one of them," she said thoughtfully after the interns left, just a hint of sadness in her voice. "Or and I had just met."

The initial few weeks of chemo went smoothly. As we'd seen with Florence, the effects of chemo are cumulative, and in the first several days Katrin said she felt terrific—in fact, more energetic than she'd felt in months because they were giving her regular blood transfusions to counter her anemia. She spent her time writing scientific papers (one of which was published by *Cell* while she was in the hospital), supervising her lab at Stanford long-distance, and buying books, toys, and winter clothes for Jake and Ella over the Internet.

Even after Katrin started feeling the effects of the chemo, she never complained, not about the Hickman line inserted into her chest that carried chemical toxins straight from a drip to her major veins ("Not bad, but I still can't look at it"); or the shivering fevers she'd suddenly get; or the hundreds of injections, pills, and needle pricks she had to endure. All the while, Katrin sent me funny e-mails that sometimes made me laugh aloud. "Yay!"

she wrote once. "Starting to feel SICK. Chemo is working . . . all according to plan." And another time: "I am looking forward to the phlebotomist visiting me this a.m. This is what I am reduced to." The phlebotomist was the person who drew her blood and told her what her blood counts were. And: "Able to drink clear fluids again. Going to try chicken broth. Yum."

I came to realize that when I didn't hear back from Katrin—when she didn't answer my calls or return my e-mails—she was either violently ill, swollen up with hives because of an allergic reaction to a platelet transfusion (something that happened regularly), or sedated with painkillers to blunt some horrible new affliction. Her updates, though, were always light-hearted. To my daily "How was last night?" e-mails, she'd respond, "You don't want to know," "Not too bad but not great at all," or "Alas, another fever."

I also realized something else: Katrin was determined to live for the sake of her children. Growing up, she'd always been the most focused of the four sisters, the one with the most concentration. Now she devoted every bit of her intellect and creativity to the task of battling her leukemia. Trained as a doctor, she was completely on top of her own disease, double-checking dosages, reviewing her cytogenetic reports, researching clinical trials on the Internet. She loved her doctors—she was medically sophisticated enough to appreciate their experience, acuity, and good judgment—and they loved her. So did all the nurses and young interns. Once, an M.D./Ph.D. student doing a rotation recognized her name—Dr. Katrin Chua of Stanford, author of two papers published in the prestigious scientific journal *Nature*!—and asked her in awe for some professional advice. Meanwhile, to stay in shape, Katrin forced herself to walk around for twenty minutes twice a day, wheeling around the IV stand she was hooked up to.

I was in Boston a lot during the fall and winter of 2008. Every weekend, our whole family would go up—sometimes we'd make the two-hour drive to Boston immediately after Lulu and I got back from our four-hour trip to Miss Tanaka. Katrin didn't care at all about having visitors herself—and after the chemo killed off her immune system, visitors were discouraged—but she was worried about Jake and Ella, and it made her happy when we spent time with them. Sophia adored her baby cousin Ella, and Lulu and Jake were best friends. They had similar personalities and looked so much alike, people often thought they were siblings.

Of course, we were all holding our breath for one thing: to see whether Katrin made it into remission. On Day 20, they took the critical biopsy. Another week passed before we got the results. They weren't good—not at all. Katrin had lost her hair, her skin was peeling, and she had every conceivable gastroenterological complication, but she was not in remission. Her doctor told her she'd need another round of chemo. "It's not the end of the world," he said, trying to sound upbeat. But we'd done our research, and we all knew that if the next round didn't work, the odds of Katrin having a successful transplant were effectively zero. It was her last chance.

28

The Sack of Rice

Sophia, age sixteen

I came home from work one evening to find a carpet of raw rice on the kitchen floor. I was tired and tense. I'd just taught, then met with students for four hours, and I was thinking about driving to Boston after dinner. A big burlap sack lay in shreds, there were rags and plastic bags all over, and Coco and Pushkin were barking up a storm outside. I knew exactly what had happened.

At that moment Sophia came into the kitchen with a broom, a distraught look on her face.

I exploded at her. "Sophia, you did it again! You left the pantry door open, didn't you? How many times have I told you the dogs would get into the rice? The entire fifty-pound bag is gone—the dogs are probably going to die now. You *never listen*. You always say, 'Oh I'm so sorry, I'll never do that again—I'm so terrible—kill me now,' but you *never change*. The only thing you care about is staying out of trouble. You have no concern for anyone else. I'm sick of you not listening—sick of it!"

Jed has always accused me of a tendency to use disproportionate force, attaching huge moral opprobrium to the smallest of oversights. But Sophia's strategy was usually just to take it and wait for the tempest to pass.

This time, however, Sophia exploded back. "Mommy! I'll clean it up, okay? You're acting like I just robbed a bank. Do you know what a good daughter I am? Everyone else I know parties all the time, and they drink and do drugs. And do you know what I do? Every day I run straight home from school. I *run*. Do you know how weird that is? I suddenly thought the other day, 'Why am I doing this? Why am I running home?' To practice more piano! You're always talking about gratitude, but you should be grateful to *me*. Don't take out your frustrations on me just because you can't control Lulu."

Sophia was completely right. She'd made me proud and my life so easy for sixteen years. But sometimes when I know I'm wrong and dislike myself, something inside me hardens and pushes me to go even further. So I said, "I never asked you to run home—that's stupid. You must look ridiculous. And if you want to do drugs, go ahead. Maybe you can meet a nice guy in Rehab."

"The dynamic in this household is ridiculous," Sophia protested. "I do all the work, and I do everything you say, and I make one mistake and you scream at me. Lulu doesn't do anything you say. She talks back to you and throws things. You bribe her with presents. What kind of 'Chinese mother' are you?"

Sophia really nailed that one. This might be a good time to raise an important point about Chinese parenting and birth order. Or maybe just birth order. I have a student named Stephanie, who recently told me a funny story. An eldest child and the daughter of Korean immigrants, Stephanie told me that when she was in high school (straight As, math whiz, concert pianist), her mother used to threaten her, "If you don't do X, I won't take you to school." And this prospect would strike terror in Stephanie's heart—miss school! So she would do whatever her mother asked, desperately hoping she wasn't too late. By contrast, when her mother threatened Stephanie's younger sister with the same thing, her sister responded, "*Awesome*. I'd love to stay home. I hate school."

There are lots of exceptions of course, but this pattern—model first kid, rebellious second—is definitely one I've noticed in many families, especially immigrant families. I just thought I could beat it in Lulu's case through sheer will and hard work.

"As you know, Sophia, I'm having trouble with Lulu," I conceded. "What worked with you isn't working with her. It's a mess."

"Oh . . . don't worry, Ma," Sophia said, her voice suddenly kind. "It's just a stage. It's awful to be thirteen—I was miserable. But things will get better."

I hadn't even known that Sophia was miserable at thirteen. Come to think of it, my mother hadn't known I was miserable at thirteen either. Like most Asian immigrant households, we didn't have heart-to-heart "talks" in my family. My mother never told me about adolescence and especially not about the gross seven-letter word that starts with *p-u* and ends with *y* and is what happens to adolescents. We absolutely never talked about the Facts of Life—just trying to imagine that conversation retroactively sends shivers up my spine.

"Sophia," I said, "you're just like I was in my family: the oldest, the one that everyone counts on and no one has to worry about. It's an honor to play that role. The problem is that Western culture doesn't see it that way. In Disney movies, the 'good daughter' always has to have a breakdown and realize that life is not all about following rules and winning prizes, and then take off her clothes and run into the ocean or something like that. But that's just Disney's way of appealing to all the people who never win any prizes. Winning prizes gives you opportunities, and that's freedom—not running into the ocean."

I was deeply moved by my oration. All the same, I felt a pang. An image of Sophia racing home from school, arms full of books, flashed into my head, and I almost couldn't take it. "Give me the broom," I said. "You need time to practice piano. I'll clean this up."

29

Despair

My sister Michelle and I were both tested to see if either of us could be Katrin's bone marrow donor. Siblings have the best chance of being a perfect match—about one in three—and I felt strangely hopeful that my blood would come through. But I was wrong. Neither Michelle nor I was a match for Katrin. The irony was that we were perfect matches for each other, but neither of us could help Katrin. This meant that Katrin now had to try to find a donor through the national bone marrow registries. To our dismay, we learned that once siblings had failed to match, the odds of finding a donor decreased dramatically, especially for people of Asian and African descent. The Internet is filled with appeals from dying patients desperately searching for a bone marrow match. And even if there was a match out there, the process could take months—months that Katrin might not have.

Katrin's first round of chemo had not been a nightmare, but

the second round more than made up for that. It was brutal. Now days would go by without my hearing from her. In panic I'd call Or, but often just get his voice mail; or he'd answer brusquely and say, "I can't talk now, Amy. I'll try to call later."

The main source of mortality from chemotherapy is infection. Ordinary ailments like the common cold or flu can easily kill a cancer patient whose white blood cells have been destroyed. Katrin got one infection after another. To fight them, her doctors prescribed a slew of antibiotics, which caused all kinds of painful side effects, and when those antibiotics didn't work, they tried different ones. She couldn't eat or drink for weeks and had to be given fluids intravenously. She was always either freezing or burning up. The complications and crises kept coming, and she was often in so much agony she had to be sedated.

When the second round of chemo had been administered, we again had to hold our breath and wait. One of the ways we'd know if Katrin's leukemia was in remission was if she starting producing healthy blood cells—in particular neutrophils, which defend against bacterial infection. I knew that Katrin's blood was drawn first thing every morning, so I'd sit at my computer screen starting at 6:00 A.M., waiting for an e-mail from her. But Katrin no longer wrote to me. When I couldn't stand waiting anymore and e-mailed Katrin first, I'd get terse answers like, "Counts not going up yet" or "Still nothing. Pretty disappointed." Soon, she didn't respond to my e-mails at all.

I've always wondered what's wrong with people who don't get the point and leave voice message after voice message ("Ca-a-ll me! Where are you? I'm worried!") even when it's obvious there's a reason no one's calling them back. Well, now I couldn't help myself. I was too anxious to care about being annoying. The week after her second round of chemo ended, I called Katrin over and over every morning, and even though she never answered—she had caller ID, so she knew it was me—I kept leaving messages, giving her updates on useless things, imagining that I was being cheery and uplifting.

Then one morning, Katrin answered the phone. She didn't sound like herself. Her voice was so faint I could barely hear her. I asked her how she was feeling, but she just sighed. Then she said, "It's no use, Amy. I'm not going to make it. There's no hope. . . . There's just no hope," and her voice trailed off.

"Don't be silly, Katrin. It's totally normal for it to take this long for counts to go up. Sometimes it can take months. Jed actually just researched all this. I can send you the numbers if you want. Also, Or tells me that the doctor is extremely optimistic. Just give it one more day."

There was no reply, so I started up again. "Lulu is such a nightmare!" I said, and I regaled her with stories about the violin and our fights and me flipping out. Before she got sick, Katrin and I had often talked about parenting and how it was impossible for us to wield the same authority over our kids that our parents had exerted over us.

Then, to my relief, I heard Katrin laugh on the other end and say in a more normal voice, "Poor Lulu. She's such a nice girl, Amy. You shouldn't be so hard on her."

On Halloween, we learned that they had located a donor, a Chinese-American who was apparently a perfect match for Katrin. Four days later, I got an e-mail from Katrin saying, "I have neutrophils! Level is 100, needs to be 500 but hopefully rising." And they did—very slowly, but they did. In early November, Katrin was released from the hospital to regain her strength. She had exactly one month before the bone marrow transplant, which unbelievably would require yet another round of chemo—this one the mother of all chemos, administered in a special germ-free ward—to wipe out all of Katrin's own diseased bone marrow so that the donor's healthy marrow could replace it. Many patients never made it out of that ward.

During her month at home, Katrin seemed so happy. She enjoyed everything: feeding Ella, taking her children for walks, and just watching them sleep. Her favorite thing was to watch Jake play tennis.

The bone marrow transplant took place on Christmas Eve. My parents and my whole family took rooms in a Boston hotel. We had takeout Chinese food and opened presents with Or, Jake, and Ella.

30

"Hebrew Melody"

A brand new year—2009. It didn't start off too festively for us. We returned from Boston, exhausted. It had been hard work trying to bring holiday cheer to Jake and Ella while their mother lay in an intensive-care bone marrow ward. Dealing with my parents was even more excruciating. My mother insisted on torturing herself by asking why, why, why Katrin had gotten leukemia. I snapped at her cruelly a few times, then felt awful. My father kept asking me the same medical questions over and over, which I referred to Jed, who patiently explained the mechanics of the transplant process. We were all terrified of what the new year might bring.

When we got back to New Haven, we found our house dark and freezing. There had been a vicious snowstorm with record-high winds, and some of our windows were broken. Then there was an electricity blackout, which left us heatless for a while. Jed and I had a new semester starting up, and courses to prepare for. Worst of all, the violin loomed—Lulu had three concerts coming up—and so did Lulu's Bat Mitzvah. Back into the trenches, I thought grimly.

Lulu and I were barely speaking. Her hair was a violent rebuke. Despite the hair cutter's best efforts, it was still short and a little jagged, and it put me in a bad mood.

In late January, Katrin was released from the hospital. She was initially so frail she had trouble going up stairs. Because she was still highly vulnerable to infection, she was not permitted to go to restaurants, grocery stores, or movie theaters without a protective mask. We all crossed our fingers and prayed that her new blood wouldn't attack her own body. We'd know within a few months whether or not she'd have the worst kind of complication—acute graft-versus-host disease—which was potentially fatal.

As the weeks passed and her Bat Mitzvah got closer, Lulu and I engaged in intensifying combat. As with Sophia, we were being unconventional and having the Bat Mitzvah in our home. Jed handled the major responsibilities, but I was the one constantly haranguing Lulu to practice her haftarah portion—I was going to be a Chinese mother even when it came to Hebrew. As always, it was over the violin that we fought most bitterly. "Didn't you hear me? I said go upstairs and practice the 'Hebrew Melody' NOW!" I must have thundered a thousand times. "It's not a difficult piece, so if it's not incredibly moving, it'll be a failure." "Do you *want* to be mediocre?" I'd yell at other times. "Is that what you want?"

Lulu always retaliated fiercely. "Not everyone's Bat Mitzvah has to be special, and I don't *want* to practice," she'd shoot back.

Or: "I'm not playing violin at my Bat Mitzvah! And you can't change my mind." Or: "I *hate* violin. I want to quit!" The decibel level in our house went off the charts. Right up until the morning of the Bat Mitzvah, I didn't know if Lulu was going to play the "Hebrew Melody" or not, even though it was on the programs Jed had had printed up.

Lulu did it. She came through. She read her Torah and haftarah portions with poise and confidence, and the way she played the "Hebrew Melody"—filling the room with tones so hauntingly beautiful guests cried—it was clear to everyone that it came from deep inside her.

At the reception afterward, I saw Lulu's face glowing as she greeted guests. "Oh my God Lulu, you are, like, *scary* on the violin, I mean like *totally amazing,*" I heard one of her friends say to her.

"She's extraordinary," a singer friend of mine marveled. "She clearly has a gift, something no one can teach." When I told her how much trouble I was having getting Lulu to practice, my friend said, "You can't let her quit. She'll regret it for the rest of her life."

That's how it always was when Lulu played the violin. Listeners were gripped by her, and she seemed gripped by the music. It's what made it so confusing and maddening when we fought and she insisted she hated the violin.

"Congratulations, Amy. Goodness knows what I could have been if you'd been *my* mother," joked our friend Caren, a former dancer. "I could have been great."

"Oh, no, Caren, I wouldn't wish myself on anyone," I said, shaking my head. "There's been a lot of yelling and screaming in this house. I didn't even think Lulu was going to play today. To tell you the truth, it's been traumatic."

"But you've given your girls so much," Caren persisted. "A sense of their own abilities, of the value of excellence. That's something they'll have all their lives."

"Maybe," I said dubiously. "I'm just not so sure anymore."

It was a great party, and everyone had fun. A big highlight was that Katrin and her family attended. In the five months since her release from the hospital, Katrin had slowly regained strength, although her immune system was still weak, and I panicked every time someone coughed. Katrin looked thin but pretty and almost triumphant carrying Ella.

That night, after all the guests had gone and we'd cleaned up as much as we could, I lay in bed wondering if Lulu might come and hug me the way she did after "The Little White Donkey." It had been a long time. But she didn't come, and I went to her bedroom instead.

"Aren't you glad I made you play the 'Hebrew Melody'?" I asked her.

Lulu seemed happy, but not particularly warm toward me. "Yes, Mommy," she said. "You can take the credit."

"Okay, I will," I said, trying to laugh. Then I told her that I was proud of her and that she'd been brilliant. Lulu smiled and was gracious. But she seemed distracted, almost impatient for me to leave, and something in her eyes told me that my days were numbered.

31

Red Square

Two days after Lulu's Bat Mitzvah, we left for Russia. It was a vacation I'd dreamed of for a long time. My parents had raved about St. Petersburg when I was a girl, and Jed and I wanted to take the girls somewhere we'd never visited ourselves.

We needed a vacation. Katrin had just passed through the worst danger zone of acute graft-versus-host disease. We'd basically gone ten months without a day's break. Our first stop was Moscow. Jed had found us a convenient hotel right in the center of the city. After a short rest, we headed out for our first taste of Russia.

I tried to be goofy and easygoing, the mood my girls most like me in, refraining as best I could from making my usual critical remarks about what they were wearing or how many times they said "like." But there was something ill-fated about that day.

It took us more than an hour standing in two different lines to change money at a place that called itself a bank, and after that the museum we wanted to visit was closed.

We decided to go to Red Square, which was within walking distance of our hotel. The sheer size of the square was overwhelming. Three football fields could have fit between the gate we entered and the onion-domed St. Basil's Cathedral at the other end. This is not a chic or charming square like the ones in Italy, I thought to myself. It's a square designed to intimidate, and I envisioned firing squads and battalions of Stalinist guards.

Lulu and Sophia kept sniping at each other, which irritated me. Actually, what really irritated me was that they were all grown up—teenagers my size (in Sophia's case, three inches taller), instead of cute little girls. "It goes so fast," older friends had always said wistfully. "Before you know it, your children will be grown and gone, and you'll be old even though you feel just like the same person you were when you were young." I never believed my friends when they said that, because it seemed to me they *were* old. By squeezing out so much from every moment of every day, perhaps I imagined that I was buying myself more time. As a purely mathematical fact, people who sleep less live more.

"That's Lenin's Tomb behind the long white wall," Jed told the girls, pointing. "His body is embalmed and on display. We can go see it tomorrow." Jed then gave the girls a short tutorial on Russian history and cold war politics.

After roaming around for a bit—we encountered surprisingly few Americans, and far more Chinese, who seemed utterly indifferent to us—we sat down at an outdoor café. It was attached to the famous GUM shopping mall, which is housed in a palatial, arcade-lined nineteenth-century building that takes up almost the entire east side of Red Square, directly across from the fortresslike Kremlin.

We decided to get blinis and caviar, a fun way to start off our first evening in Moscow, Jed and I thought. But when the caviar arrived—thirty U.S. dollars for a tiny receptacle—Lulu said, "Eww, gross," and wouldn't try it.

"Sophia, don't take so much; leave some for the rest of us," I snapped, then turned to my other daughter. "Lulu, you sound like an uncultured savage. Try the caviar. You can put a lot of sour cream on it."

"That's even worse," Lulu said, and she made a shuddering gesture. "And don't call me a savage."

"Don't wreck the vacation for everyone, Lulu."

"You're the one wrecking it."

I pushed the caviar toward Lulu. I ordered her to try one egg—one single egg.

"Why?" Lulu asked defiantly. "Why do you care so much? You can't force me to eat something."

I felt my temper rising. Could I not get Lulu to do even one tiny thing? "You're behaving like a juvenile delinquent. *Try one egg now.*"

"I don't want to," said Lulu.

"*Do it now,* Lulu."

"No."

"Amy," Jed began diplomatically, "everyone's tired. Why don't we just—"

I broke in, "Do you know how sad and ashamed my parents would be if they saw this, Lulu—you publicly disobeying me?

With that look on your face? You're only hurting yourself. We're in Russia, and you refuse to try caviar! You're like a barbarian. And in case you think you're a big rebel, you are *completely ordinary*. There is nothing more typical, more predictable, more common and low, than an American teenager who won't try things. You're boring, Lulu—*boring*."

"Shut up," said Lulu angrily.

"Don't you dare say shut up to me. I'm your mother." I hissed this, but still a few guests glanced over. "Stop trying to act tough to impress Sophia."

"I *hate* you! I HATE YOU." This, from Lulu, was not in a hiss. It was an all-out shout at the top of her lungs. Now the entire café was staring at us.

"You don't love me," Lulu spat out. "You think you do, but you don't. You just make me feel bad about myself every second. You've wrecked my life. I can't stand to be around you. Is that what you want?"

A lump rose in my throat. Lulu saw it, but she went on. "You're a *terrible mother*. You're selfish. You don't care about anyone but yourself. What—you can't believe how ungrateful I am? After all you've done for me? Everything you say you do for me is actually for yourself."

She's just like me, I thought, compulsively cruel. "You are a terrible daughter," I said aloud.

"I know—I'm not what you want—I'm not Chinese! I don't want to be Chinese. Why can't you get that through your head? I *hate* the violin. I HATE my life. I HATE you, and I HATE this family! I'm going to take this glass and smash it!"

"Do it," I dared.

Lulu grabbed a glass from the table and threw it on the

ground. Water and shards went flying, and some guests gasped. I felt all eyes upon us, a grotesque spectacle.

I'd made a career out of spurning the kind of Western parents who can't control their kids. Now I had the most disrespectful, rude, violent, out-of-control kid of all.

Lulu was trembling with rage, and there were tears in her eyes. "I'll smash more if you don't leave me alone," she cried.

I got up and ran. I ran as fast as I could, not knowing where I was going, a crazy forty-six-year-old woman sprinting in sandals and crying. I ran past Lenin's mausoleum and past some guards with guns who I thought might shoot me.

Then I stopped. I had come to the end of Red Square. There was nowhere to go.

32

The Symbol

Families often have symbols: a lake in the country, Grandpa's medal, the Sabbath dinner. In our household, the violin had become a symbol.

For me, it symbolized excellence, refinement, and depth—the opposite of shopping malls, megasized Cokes, teenage clothes, and crass consumerism. Unlike listening to an iPod, playing the violin is difficult and requires concentration, precision, and interpretation. Even physically, everything about the violin—the burnished wood, the carved scroll, the horsehair, the delicate bridge, the sounding point—is subtle, exquisite, and precarious.

To me, the violin symbolized respect for hierarchy, standards, and expertise. For those who know better and can teach. For those who play better and can inspire. And for parents.

It also symbolized history. The Chinese never achieved the heights of Western classical music—there is no Chinese equivalent of Beethoven's Ninth Symphony—but high traditional music is deeply entwined with Chinese civilization. The seven-stringed *qin,* often associated with Confucius, has been around for at least twenty-five hundred years. It was immortalized by the great Tang poets, revered as the instrument of the sages.

Most of all, the violin symbolized control. Over generational decline. Over birth order. Over one's destiny. Over one's children. Why should the grandchildren of immigrants only be able to play the guitar or drums? Why should second children so predictably be less rule-abiding, less successful at school, and "more social" than eldest siblings? In short, the violin symbolized the success of the Chinese parenting model.

For Lulu, it embodied oppression.

And as I walked slowly back across Red Square, I realized that the violin had begun to symbolize oppression for me too. Just picturing Lulu's violin case sitting at home by the front door—at the last minute we'd decided to leave it behind, the first time ever—made me think of the hours and hours and years and years of labor, fighting, aggravation, and misery that we'd endured. For what? I also realized that I was dreading with all my heart what lay ahead.

It occurred to me that this must be how Western parents think and why they so often let their kids give up difficult musical instruments. Why torture yourself and your child? What's the point? If your child doesn't like something—hates it—what good is it forcing her to do it? I knew as a Chinese mother I could never give in to that way of thinking.

I rejoined my family at the GUM café. The waiters and other guests averted their eyes.

"Lulu," I said. "You win. It's over. We're giving up the violin."

33

Going West

My Dad, early 1970s

I wasn't bluffing. I'd always engaged in brinkmanship with Lulu, but this time I was serious. I'm still not exactly sure why. Maybe I finally allowed myself to admire Lulu's immovable strength for what it was, even if I bitterly disagreed with her choices. Or maybe it was Katrin. Watching her struggle and seeing what became important to her in those desperate months shook things up for all of us.

It could also have been my mother. To me, she'll always be

the quintessential Chinese mother. Growing up, nothing was ever good enough for her. ("You say you got first place, but actually you only tied for first, right?") She used to practice piano with Cindy three hours a day until the teacher gently told her that they'd hit a limit. Even after I became a professor and invited her to some of my public lectures, she always offered painfully accurate criticisms while everyone else was telling me what a good job I'd done. ("You get too excited and talk too fast. Try to stay cool, and you'll be better.") Yet my own Chinese mother had been warning me for a long time that something wasn't working with Lulu. "Every child is different," she said. "You have to adjust, Amy. Look what happened to your father," she added ominously.

So—about my father. I guess it's time to come clean with something. I'd always told Jed, myself, and everyone else that the ultimate proof of the superiority of Chinese parenting is how the children end up feeling about their parents. Despite their parents' brutal demands, verbal abuse, and disregard for their children's desires, Chinese kids end up adoring and respecting their parents and wanting to care for them in their old age. From the beginning, Jed had always asked, "What about your dad, Amy?" I'd never had a good answer.

My father was the black sheep in his family. His mother disfavored him and treated him unfairly. In his household, comparisons among the children were common, and my father—the fourth of six—was always on the short end of the stick. He wasn't interested in business like the rest of his family. He loved science and fast cars; at age eight, he built a radio from scratch. Compared to his siblings, my father was the family outlaw, risk-taking and rebellious. To put it mildly, his mother didn't respect his choices, value his individualism, or worry about his self-esteem—all those Western clichés. The result was that my father hated his family—found it suffocating and undermining—and as soon as he had a chance he moved as far away as he could, never once looking back.

What my father's story illustrates is something I suppose I never wanted to think about. When Chinese parenting succeeds, there's nothing like it. But it doesn't always succeed. For my own father it hadn't. He barely spoke to his mother and never thought about her except in anger. By the end of her life, my father's family was almost dead to him.

I couldn't lose Lulu. Nothing was more important. So I did the most Western thing imaginable: I gave *her* the choice. I told her that she could quit the violin if she wanted and do what she liked instead, which at the time was to play tennis.

At first, Lulu assumed it was a trap. Over the years, the two of us had played so many games of chicken and engaged in such elaborate forms of psychological warfare that she was naturally suspicious. But when Lulu realized I was sincere, she surprised me.

"I don't want to quit," she said. "I love the violin. I would never give it up."

"Oh please," I said, shaking my head. "Let's not go in circles again."

"I don't want to quit violin," Lulu repeated. "I just don't want to be so intense about it. It's not the main thing I want to do with my life. You picked it, not me."

It turns out that not being intense had some radical, and for me heartbreaking, implications. First, Lulu decided to quit orchestra, giving up her concertmaster position in order to free up Saturday mornings for tennis. Not a second goes by that this doesn't cause me pain. When she played her last piece as concertmaster at a recital at Tanglewood and then shook the conductor's hand, I almost wept. Second, Lulu decided that she didn't want to go to New York every Sunday for violin lessons anymore, so we gave up our spot in Miss Tanaka's studio—our precious spot with a famous Juilliard teacher that had been so hard to get!

Instead, I found Lulu a local teacher in New Haven. After a long talk, we also agreed that Lulu would practice by herself, without me or regular coaches, and for just thirty minutes a day—not nearly enough, I knew, to maintain her high level of playing.

For the first few weeks after Lulu's decision, I wandered around the house like a person who'd lost their mission, their reason for living.

At a recent lunch, I met Elizabeth Alexander, the Yale professor who read her original poem at President Obama's inauguration. I told her how much I admired her work, and we exchanged a few words.

Then she said, "Wait a minute—I think I know you. Do you have two daughters who studied at the Neighborhood Music School? Aren't you the mother of those two incredibly talented musicians?"

It turns out that Elizabeth had two kids, younger than mine, who studied at the Neighborhood Music School also, and they'd heard Sophia and Lulu perform on several occasions. "Your daughters are *amazing*," she said.

In the old days, I would have said modestly, "Oh they're really not that good," hoping desperately that she'd ask me more so I could tell her about Sophia's and Lulu's latest music accomplishments. Now I just shook my head.

"Do they still play?" Elizabeth continued. "I don't see them at the school anymore."

"My older daughter still plays piano," I replied. "My younger daughter—the violinist—she doesn't really play so much anymore." This was like a knife to my heart. "She prefers to play tennis instead." Even if she is ranked #10,000 in New England, I thought to myself. Out of 10,000.

"Oh no!" Elizabeth said. "That's too bad. I remember she was so gifted. She inspired my two little ones."

"It was her decision," I heard myself saying. "It was too much of a time commitment. You know how thirteen-year-olds are." What a Western parent I've become, I thought to myself. What a failure.

But I kept my word. I let Lulu play tennis as she pleased, at her own pace, making her own decisions. I remember the first time she signed herself up for a Novice USTA tournament. She came back in a good mood, visibly charged with adrenaline.

"How did you do?" I asked.

"Oh, I lost—but it was my first tournament, and my strategy was all wrong."

"What was the score?"

"Love-six, love-six," Lulu said. "But the girl I played was really good."

If she's so good, why is she playing in a Novice tournament? I thought darkly to myself, but aloud I said, "Bill Clinton recently told some Yale students that you can only be really great at something if you love it. So it's good that you love tennis."

But just because you love something, I added to myself, doesn't mean you'll ever be great. Not if you don't work. Most people stink at the things they love.

34

The Ending

Lulu on court

We recently hosted a formal dinner at our home for judges from all over the world. One of the most humbling things about being a Yale law professor is that you get to meet some awe-inspiring figures—some of the greatest jurists of the day. For ten years now, Yale's global constitutionalism seminar has brought in supreme court justices from dozens of countries, including the United States.

For entertainment, we invited Sophia's piano professor, Wei-

Yi Yang, to perform part of the program he was preparing for Yale's famous Horowitz Piano Series. Wei-Yi generously suggested that his young pupil Sophia perform as well. For fun, teacher and student could also play a duet together: "En Bateau" from Debussy's *Petite Suite*.

I was incredibly excited and nervous about the idea and nurturingly said to Sophia, "Don't blow this. Everything turns on your performance. The justices aren't coming to New Haven to hear a high school talent show. If you're not over-the-top perfect we'll have insulted them. Now go to the piano and don't leave it." I guess there's still a bit of the Chinese mother in me.

The next few weeks were like a replay of the run-up to Carnegie Hall, except that now Sophia did almost all her practicing herself. As in the past, I immersed myself in her pieces—Saint-Saëns's *Allegro Appassionato* and a polonaise and *Fantaisie Impromptu* by Chopin—but the truth was that Sophia barely needed me anymore. She knew exactly what she had to do, and only occasionally would I yell out a critique from the kitchen or upstairs. Meanwhile, Jed and I had all our living room furniture moved out except the piano. I scrubbed the floor myself, and we rented chairs for fifty people.

The evening of the performance Sophia wore a red dress, and as she walked in to take her opening bow, panic seized me. I was practically frozen during the polonaise. I couldn't enjoy the Saint-Saëns either, even though Sophia played it brilliantly. That piece is meant to be sheer virtuosic entertainment, and I was too tense to be entertained. Could Sophia keep her runs sparkling and clean? Had she overpracticed, and would her hands give out? I had to force myself not to rock and back forth and hum robotically, which is what I usually do when the girls perform a difficult piece.

Lakdja

But when Sophia played her last piece, Chopin's *Fantaisie Impromptu,* everything changed. For some reason, the tension in me dissipated, the lockjaw released, and all I could think was, She owns this piece. When she got up to take her bow, a radiant smile on her face, I thought, That's my girl—she's happy; the music is making her happy. Right then I knew that it had all been worth it.

Sophia received three ovations, and afterward the justices—including many I've idolized for years—were effusive in their praise. One said Sophia's playing was sublime and that he could have listened to her all night. Another insisted that she had to pursue the piano professionally because it would be a crime to waste her talent. And a surprising number of the justices, being parents themselves, asked me personal questions like, "What is your secret? Do you think it's something about the Asian family culture that tends to produce so many exceptional musicians?" Or: "Tell me: Does Sophia practice on her own because she loves music or do you have to force her? I could never make my own children practice more than fifteen minutes." And: "How about your other daughter? I hear she's a fabulous violinist. Will we hear her next time?"

I told them that I was struggling to finish a book on just those questions and that I would send them a copy when it was done.

Around the same time as Sophia's performance for the justices, I picked Lulu up from some godforsaken tennis place in Connecticut about an hour away.

"Guess what, Mommy—I won!"

"Won what?" I asked.

"The tournament," Lulu said.

"What does that mean?"

"I won three matches, and I beat the top seed in the finals. She was ranked #60 in New England. I can't believe I beat her!"

This took me aback. I'd played tennis as a teenager myself, but always just for fun with my family or school friends. As an adult, I tried a few tournaments but quickly found that I couldn't stand the pressure of competition. Mainly so we could have a family activity, Jed and I had made both Sophia and Lulu take tennis lessons, but we'd never had any hopes.

"Are you still playing at the Novice level?" I asked Lulu. "The lowest level?"

"Yes," she answered amiably. Ever since I'd given her the choice, we'd gotten along much better. My pain seemed to be her gain, and she was more patient and good-humored. "But I'm going to try the next level soon. I'm sure I'll lose, but I want to try it for fun."

And then, out of the blue: "I miss orchestra so much," Lulu said.

Over the next six weeks, Lulu won three more tournaments. At the last two, I went to watch her play. I was struck by what a fireball she was on the court: how fiercely she hit, how concentrated she looked, and how she never gave up.

As Lulu notched herself up, the competition got much tougher. At one tournament, she lost to a girl twice her size. When Lulu came off the court, she was smiling and gracious, but the second she got in the car she said to me, "I'm going to beat her next time. I'm not good enough yet—but soon." Then she asked me if I could sign her up for extra tennis lessons.

At the next lesson, I watched Lulu drill her backhand with a focus and tenacity I'd never seen in her. Afterward, she asked me if I would feed her more balls so that she could keep practicing, and we went for another hour. On the way home, when I told her how much better her backhand looked, she said, "*No,* it's not right yet. It's still terrible. Can we get a court tomorrow?"

She's so driven, I thought to myself. So . . . intense.

I talked to Lulu's tennis instructor. "There's no way Lulu can ever be really good, right? I mean, she's thirteen—that's got to be ten years too late." I'd heard about the explosion of high-powered tennis academies and four-year-olds with personal trainers. "Also, she's so short, like me."

"The important thing is that Lulu loves tennis," the instructor said, very American-ly. "And she has an unbelievable work ethic—I've never seen anyone improve so fast. She's a great kid. You and your husband have done an amazing job with her. She never settles for less than 110 percent. And she's always so upbeat and polite."

"You've got to be kidding," I said. But despite myself, my spirits lifted. Could this be the Chinese virtuous circle in action? Had I perhaps just chosen the wrong activity for Lulu? Tennis was very respectable—it wasn't like bowling. Michael Chang had played tennis.

I started to gear up. I familiarized myself with the USTA rules and procedures and the national ranking system. I also looked into trainers and started calling around about the best tennis clinics in the area.

Lulu overheard me one day. "What are you doing?" she demanded. When I explained that I was just doing a little research, she suddenly got furious. "No, Mommy—*no!*" she said fiercely. "Don't wreck tennis for me like you wrecked violin."

That really hurt. I backed off.

The next day I tried again. "Lulu, there's a place in Massachusetts—"

"No, Mommy—please stop," Lulu said. "I can do this on my own. I don't need you to be involved."

"Lulu, what we need to do is to channel your strength—"

"Mommy, I *get it*. I've watched you and listened to your lectures a million times. But I don't want you controlling my life."

I focused my eyes on Lulu, taking her in. Everyone had always said she looked just like me, something that I loved to hear but that she vehemently denied. An image of her at age three standing outside, defiant in the cold, came to my mind. She's indomitable, I thought to myself, and always has been. Wherever she ends up, she's going to be amazing.

"Okay, Lulu, I can accept that," I said. "See how undefensive and flexible I am? To succeed in this world, you always have to be willing to adapt. That's something I'm especially good at that you should learn from me."

But I didn't really give up. I'm still in the fight, albeit with some significant modifications to my strategy. I've become newly accepting and open-minded. The other day Lulu told me she would have even less time for violin because she wanted to pursue other interests, like writing and "improv." Instead of choking, I was supportive and proactive. I'm taking the long view. Lulu can do side-splitting imitations, and while improv does seems un-Chinese and the opposite of classical music, it is definitely a skill. I also harbor hopes that Lulu won't be able to escape her love of music and that someday—maybe soon—she'll return to the violin of her own accord.

Meanwhile, every weekend, I drive Lulu to tennis tournaments and watch her play. She recently made the high school varsity team, the only middle school kid to do so. Because Lulu has insisted that she wants no advice or criticism from me, I've resorted to espionage and guerrilla warfare. I secretly plant ideas in her tennis coach's head, texting her with questions and practice strategies, then deleting the text messages so Lulu won't see them. Sometimes, when Lulu's least expecting it—at breakfast or when I'm saying good night—I'll suddenly yell out, "More rotation on the swing volley!" or "Don't move your right foot on your kick serve!" And Lulu will plug her ears, and we'll fight, but I'll have gotten my message out, and I know she knows I'm right.

Coda

Our family, 2010

Tigers are passionate and rash, blinding themselves
to danger. But they draw on experience, gaining new
energies and great strength.

I started writing this book on June 29, 2009, the day after we
got back from Russia. I didn't know why I was doing it or how
the book was going to end, but even though I usually have writer's block, this time the words streamed out of me. The first
two-thirds of the book took me just eight weeks to write. (The

last third was agonizing.) I showed every page to Jed and the girls. "We're writing this together," I said to Sophia and Lulu.

"No, we're not," they both said. "It's your book, Mommy, not ours."

"I'm sure it's all about you anyway," added Lulu.

But as time went on, the more the girls read, the more they contributed. The truth is, it's been therapeutic—a Western concept, the girls remind me.

I'd forgotten a lot of things over the years, good and bad, which the girls and Jed helped me remember. To try to piece things together, I dug up old e-mails, computer files, music programs, and photo albums. Often, Jed and I were overcome with nostalgia. Sophia was just a baby yesterday, it seemed, and now she was a year away from applying to college. Sophia and Lulu were mainly overcome with how cute they used to be.

Don't get me wrong: Writing this book hasn't been easy. Nothing in our family ever is. I had to produce multiple drafts, revising constantly to address the girls' objections. I ended up leaving out big chunks about Jed, because that's a whole other book, and it's really his story to tell. Some parts I had to rewrite two dozen times before I could satisfy both Sophia and Lulu. On several occasions, one of them would be reading a draft chapter, then suddenly burst into tears and storm off. Or I'd get a curt, "This is great, Ma, very funny. I just don't know who you're writing about, that's all. It's definitely not *our* family."

"Oh no!" Lulu cried out once. "Am I supposed to be Pushkin, the dumb one? And Sophia is Coco, who's smart and learns everything?" I pointed out that Coco wasn't smart and couldn't learn anything either. I assured the girls that the dogs weren't supposed to be metaphors for them.

"So what purpose are they serving?" Sophia asked, ever logical. "Why are they in the book?"

"I don't know yet," I admitted. "But I know they're important. There's something inherently unstable about a Chinese mother raising dogs."

Another time, Lulu complained, "I think you're exaggerating the difference between Sophia and me to try to make the book interesting. You make me sound like a typical rebellious American teenager, when I'm not even close." Sophia, meanwhile, had just said, "I think you tone down Lulu too much. You make her sound like an angel."

Naturally, both girls felt the book shortchanged them. "You should definitely dedicate this book to Lulu," Sophia once said magnanimously. "She's obviously the heroine. I'm the boring one readers will cheer against. She's the one with *verve* and *panache*." And from Lulu: "Maybe you should call your book *The Perfect Child and the Flesh-Eating Devil*. Or *Why Oldest Children Are Better*. That's what it's about, right?"

As the summer went on, the girls never stopped nagging me, "So how's the book going to end, Mommy? Is it going to be a happy ending?"

I'd always say something like, "It depends on you guys. But I'm guessing it'll be a tragedy."

Months passed, but I just couldn't figure out how to end the book. Once, I came running up to the girls. "I've got it! I'm about to finish the book."

The girls were excited. "So how will it end?" Sophia asked. "What's your point going to be?"

"I've decided to favor a hybrid approach," I said. "The best of both worlds. The Chinese way until the child is eighteen, to develop confidence and the value of excellence, then the Western way after that. Every individual has to find their own path," I added gallantly.

"Wait—until eighteen?" asked Sophia. "That's not a hybrid approach. That's just Chinese parenting all through childhood."

"I think you're being too technical, Sophia."

Nevertheless, I went back to the drawing board. I spun more wheels, cranked out some more duds. Finally, one day— actually yesterday—I asked the girls how *they* thought the book should end.

"Well," said Sophia, "are you trying to tell the truth in this book or just a good story?"

"The truth," I replied.

"That's going to be hard, because the truth keeps changing," said Sophia.

"No it doesn't," I said. "I have a perfect memory."

"Then why do you keep revising the ending all the time?" asked Sophia.

"Because she doesn't know what she wants to say," Lulu offered.

"It's not possible for you to tell the complete truth," said Sophia. "You've left out so many facts. But that means no one can really understand. For example, everyone's going to think that I was *subjected* to Chinese parenting, but I wasn't. I went along with it, by my own choice."

"Not when you were little," Lulu said. "Mommy never gave us a choice when we were little. Unless it was, 'Do you want to practice six hours or five?'"

"Choice . . . I wonder if that's what it all comes down to," I mused. "Westerners believe in choice; the Chinese don't. I used to make fun of Popo for giving Daddy a choice about violin lessons. Of course he chose not to. But now, Lulu, I wonder what would have happened if I hadn't forced you to audition for Juilliard or practice so many hours a day. Who knows? Maybe you'd still like violin. Or what if I'd let you choose your own instrument? Or no instrument? After all, Daddy turned out fine."

"Don't be ridiculous," said Lulu. "Of course I'm glad you forced me to play the violin."

"Oh, *right*. Hello Dr. Jekyll! Where's Mr. Hyde?"

"No—I mean it," Lulu said. "I'm always going to love the violin. I'm even glad you made me drill exponents. And study Chinese for two hours every day."

"Seriously?" I asked.

"Yeah," nodded Lulu.

"Really!" I said. "Because come to think of it, I think those were great choices we made too, even though all those people worried that you and Sophia would be permanently damaged psychologically. And you know, the more I think about it, the madder I'm getting. All these Western parents with the same party line about what's good for children and what's not—I'm not sure they're making choices at all. They just do what everyone else does. They're not questioning anything either, which is what Westerners are supposed to be so good at doing. They just keep repeating things like 'You have to give your children the freedom to pursue their *passion*' when it's obvious that the 'passion' is just going to turn out to be Facebook for ten hours which is a total waste of time and eating all that disgusting junk food—I'm telling you this country is going to go *straight down-*

hill! No wonder Western parents get thrown into nursing homes when they're old! You guys better not put me in one of those. And I don't want my plug pulled either."

"Calm down, Mommy," said Lulu.

"When their kids fail at something, instead of telling them to work harder, the first thing Western parents do is bring a lawsuit!"

"Who exactly are you talking about?" asked Sophia. "I don't know any Western parents who have brought a lawsuit."

"I refuse to buckle to politically correct Western social norms that are obviously stupid. And not even rooted historically. What are the origins of the Playdate anyway? Do you think our Founding Fathers had Sleepovers? I actually think America's Founding Fathers had Chinese values."

"I hate to break it to you, Mommy, but—"

"Ben Franklin said, 'If thou loveth life, never ever EVER wasteth time.' Thomas Jefferson said, 'I'm a huge believer in luck, and the harder I work the more I have of it.' And Alexander Hamilton said, 'Don't be a whiner.' That's a totally Chinese way of thinking."

"Mommy, if the Founding Fathers thought that way, then it's an American way of thinking," said Sophia. "Besides, I think you may be misquoting."

"Look it up," I dared her.

My sister Katrin is doing better now. Life is definitely tough for her, and she's not out of the woods yet, but she's a hero and bears everything with grace, doing research around the clock, writing paper after paper, and spending as much time as she can with her kids.

I often wonder what the lesson of her illness is. Given that life is so short and so fragile, surely each of us should be trying to get the most out of every breath, every fleeting moment. But what does it mean to live life to its fullest?

We all have to die. But which way does that cut? In any case, I've just told Jed that I want to get another dog.

Acknowledgments

I have so many people to thank:

My mother and father—no one has believed in me more, and they have my deepest admiration and gratitude.

Sophia and Louisa, my greatest source of happiness, the pride and joy of my life.

My extraordinary sisters, Michelle, Katrin, and Cindy.

And most of all, my husband, Jed Rubenfeld, who for twenty-five years has read every word I've written. I am the unbelievably lucky beneficiary of his kindness and genius.

My brother-in-law Or Gozani and my nieces and nephews Amalia, Dimitri, Diana, Jake, and Ella.

The following dear friends, for insightful comments, passionate debates, and invaluable support: Alexis Contant and Jordan Smoller, Sylvia and Walter Austerer, Susan and Paul Fiedler, Marina Santilli, Anne Dailey, Jennifer Brown (for "humbled"!),

Nancy Greenberg, Anne Tofflemire, Sarah Bilston and Daniel Markovits, and Kathleen Brown-Dorato and Alex Dorato. Thanks also to Elizabeth Alexander, Barbara Rosen, Roger Spottiswoode, Emily Bazelon, Linda Burt, and Annie Witt for their generous encouragement.

All those who helped instill the love of music in Sophia and Lulu, including Michelle Zingale, Carl Shugart, Fiona Murray, Jody Rowitsch, and Alexis Zingale of the Neighborhood Music School; the fabulous Richard Brooks of the Norwalk Youth Symphony; Annette Chang Barger, Ying Ying Ho, Yu-ting Huang, Nancy Jin, Kiwon Nahm, and Alexandra Newman; the exceptional Naoko Tanaka and Almita Vamos; and especially my good friend, the incomparable Wei-Yi Yang.

All of the wonderful teachers Sophia and Lulu were lucky enough to have at the Foote School (and I actually loved the Medieval Festival), especially Judy Cuthbertson and Cliff Sahlin.

On the tennis front: Alex Dorato, Christian Appleman, and Stacia Fonseca.

My students Jacqueline Esai, Ronan Farrow, Sue Guan, Stephanie Lee, Jim Ligtenberg, Justin Lo, Peter McElligott, Luke Norris, Amelia Rawls, Nabiha Syed, and Elina Tetelbaum.

Finally, my heartfelt thanks to the amazing Tina Bennett, the best agent imaginable, and to my editor and publisher, the brilliant, unsurpassed Ann Godoff.

Notes

The Chinese zodiac Tiger epigrams are from "Chinese Zodiac: Tiger," http://pages.infinit.net/garrick/chinese/tiger.html (visited December 18, 2009), and "Chinese Zodiac: Tiger," http://www.chinesezodiac.com/tiger.php (visited December 18, 2009).

Chapter 1: The Chinese Mother

The statistics I cite are from the following studies: Ruth K. Chao, "Chinese and European American Mothers' Beliefs About the Role of Parenting in Children's School Success," *Journal of Cross-Cultural Psychology* 27 (1996): 403–23; Paul E. Jose, Carol S. Huntsinger, Phillip R. Huntsinger, and Fong-Ruey Liaw, "Parental Values and Practices Relevant to Young Children's Social Development in Taiwan and the United States," *Journal of Cross-Cultural Psychology* 31 (2000): 677–702; and Parminder Parmar, "Teacher or Playmate? Asian Immigrant and Euro-American Parents' Participation in Their Young Children's Daily Activities," *Social Behavior and Personality* 36(2) (2008): 163–76.

Chapter 3: Louisa

The country music song I quote is "Wild One," written by Jaime Kyle, Pat Bunch, and Will Rambeaux. My Chinese zodiac characteristics come from the following Web sites: "Monkey Facts," http://www.chineseinkdesign.com/Chinese-Zodiac-

Monkey.html (visited December 18, 2009); "The Pig/Boar Personality," http://
www.chinavoc.com/zodiac/pig/person.asp (visited December 18, 2009); and
"Chinese Zodiac: Tiger," http://pages.infinit.net/garrick/chinese/tiger.html
(visited December 18, 2009).

Chapter 5: On Generational Decline
For an illuminating study of Asian "music moms," see Grace Wang, "Interlopers in
the Realm of High Culture: 'Music Moms' and the Performance of Asian and
Asian American Identities," *American Quarterly* 61(4) (2009): 881–903.

Chapter 8: Lulu's Instrument
Brent Hugh, "Claude Debussy and the Javanese Gamelan," available at http://
brenthugh.com/debnotes/debussy-gamelan.pdf (visited December 12, 2009)
(script for a lecture recital given at the University of Missouri–Kansas City
in 1998).

Chapter 9: The Violin
On how to hold the violin, see Carl Flesch, *The Art of Violin Playing, Book One,*
trans. and ed. Eric Rosenblith (New York: Carl Fischer, 2000), 3.

Chapter 12: The Cadenza
On Asian overrepresentation at top music schools:

> At leading music schools and departments, Asians and Asian Amer-
> icans constitute from 30 to 50 percent of the student population.
> The numbers are often higher at the pre-college level. At highly
> regarded programs such as Juilliard Pre-College, Asians and Asian
> Americans compose more than half the student body; the two larg-
> est groups represented are students of Chinese and Korean descent
> studying the violin or piano.

Grace Wang, "Interlopers in the Realm of High Culture: 'Music Moms' and the
Performance of Asian and Asian American Identities," *American Quarterly* 61(4)
(2009): 882.

Chapter 13: Coco
On Dr. Stanley Coren and his rankings, see "The Intelligence of Dogs," available
at http://petrix.com/dogint/ (visited July 24, 2009). Other sources I cite:

Michael D. Jones, "Samoyeds Breed—FAQ" (1997), available at http://www .faqs.org/faqs/dogs-faq/breeds/samoyeds/ (visited July 21, 2009); and SnowAngels Samoyeds, "The Samoyed Dog: A Short History," available at http:// www.snowangelssamoyeds.com/The_Samoyed.html (visited July 21, 2009) (italics added).

A Note on the Author

Amy Chua is the John M. Duff Professor of Law at Yale Law School. Her first book, *World on Fire: How Exporting Free Market Democracy Breeds Ethnic Hatred and Global Instability*, translated into eight languages, was a *New York Times* bestseller, an *Economist* Best Book of the Year, and one of the *Guardian*'s Top Political Reads of 2003. Her second book, *Day of Empire: How Hyperpowers Rise to Global Dominance — and Why They Fall*, was a critically acclaimed *Foreign Affairs* bestseller. Amy Chua has appeared frequently on radio and television and her writing has been published in the *New York Times*, the *Washington Post*, the *Financial Times*, *Harvard Business Review*, and the *Wilson Quarterly*. She lives with her husband, two daughters, and two Samoyeds in New Haven, Connecticut.

A Note on the Type

The text of this book is set in Perpetua. This typeface is an adaptation of a style of letter that had been popularized for monumental work in stone by Eric Gill. Large scale drawings by Gill were given to Charles Malin, a Parisian punch-cutter, and his hand cut punches were the basis for the font issued by Monotype. First used in a private translation called *The Passion of Perpetua and Felicity*, the italic was originally called Felicity.